For my mother who first
took me abroad, my children
Liza, Henry and Kate, and
my travelling companions
David, Elizabeth and Johnny.

Quadrille
PUBLISHING

Josceline Dimbleby

Orchards in the Oasis

Recipes, Travels & Memories

Recipe photographs
by Jason Lowe

Contents

Notes on using the recipes

Use fresh herbs, sea salt and freshly ground pepper unless otherwise listed.

Timings are for conventional ovens. If using a fan-assisted oven, reduce the setting by 15°C (1 Gas mark). Ovens vary considerably, so please check towards the end of cooking and rely on your own judgement.

Introduction

When you study an old photograph for several minutes, examining every detail, the image seems to come alive. If you also have a diary relating to when the picture was taken, lost memories vividly return – of places, people, adventures, surprises, and one of life's greatest pleasures, food. This is what happened to me when I began to plan this book, looking back through my photograph albums, which cover a period of sixty years, and re-reading diaries, travel notebooks, letters and hundreds of recipes.

After a childhood spent mostly abroad because my stepfather was in the diplomatic service, I became a compulsive traveller, letter and diary writer, photographer – and eater. I have always diligently stuck my photographs in albums – there are so many now that I no longer have shelves left for them – and kept all negatives in dated and named files. As I gathered together the albums and dug out all my old diaries and notebooks I realised what a mass of material I had after all these years, and was faced with a bewildering choice. So many countries and cultures had fascinated, moved or amused me, and together with key times at home, shaped my cooking.

I searched for the best stories from parts of the world especially important to me, and places where the food I ate had made the deepest impression. Once again I cooked dishes inspired by past experiences, and the smells and tastes made me feel I had travelled back in time. So here are moments throughout my life in far-off countries and at home, illustrated with contemporary images from my albums, and by Jason Lowe's beautiful photographs of favourite relevant recipes, revised and cooked in my present-day London kitchen. It has been as good as any journey I have made, and one I shall never forget.

a child in Damascus

ccompanied by a middle-aged governess I barely knew, I had been travelling by cargo ship on a rough sea for five days from England to the Lebanon, followed by a hot dusty drive over the mountains into Syria. I was only seven years old. Tired, thirsty and bewildered, I clutched my rag doll Alice and a tiny bear called Little Mut. At last, in the valley below, we saw Damascus, where I knew I would be reunited with my mother, who had arrived earlier by a Pan American Airways Constellation, often called the lion of the sky. From the mountains above, the ancient city looked like an illustration for a fairy story; encircled by the desert hills, its domes and minarets nestled in an oasis of poplars and fruit orchards, irrigated by sparkling streams fed by a shimmering river, the Barada.

Once in the city there were trams and horse-drawn gharries carrying passengers, but few cars. Groups of men sat in cafés smoking hubble-bubble pipes; they wore Turkish style red fezes and *cheroual* – capacious trousers, tight at the ankle, ready for the birth of the second Messiah, supposedly to a man. Finally we reached a large white house with blue shutters and pointed Arab windows and I ran into my mother's arms. A pale, thin-faced man with ripply black hair, a neat moustache and

kind eyes stood nearby holding a tray. He smiled at me and asked if I would like a glass of deep scarlet juice. 'This is Khalil, our butler,' said Barbara, my mother, 'and that's pomegranate juice from the fruit in the garden.' The juice was delicious. Suddenly refreshed, I ran across the marble floor through some doors at the end and into the most magical garden I had ever seen. There were paved paths and lawns, and an orchard at the far end with olive, lemon and little mulberry trees. Criss-crossing the whole garden were irrigation streams, so that everything was a fresh green despite the summer heat. Dark pink roses seemed to be everywhere and I could smell their scent. In the middle of the main lawn was a statuesque old walnut tree whose contorted branches made a pattern of shadows on the velvety carpet of green as the sun shone fiercely down. Something white fluttered past me and I noticed a wooden dovecot to one side of the house.

My stepfather had been posted as Minister at the British Legation in Damascus, so our house (pictured left) came complete with servants, including the butler Khalil (pictured left), who ultimately worked for the British for thirty years, and Joseph, an Armenian cook who was helped by a huge 'cook's boy'. The 'boy' was about forty and known as 'the marmiton', since he had previously worked for the French. As soon as Khalil showed me the kitchen I knew it was a place I would often be in. Joseph was as friendly as Khalil, and

Pyramids of pastries in a Damascene sweet shop.

the marmiton laughed when I asked if the seeds he was grinding with a stone were for the garden. 'They're spices from the souk,' Khalil told me, 'you'll see them tomorrow.' Beside the spices was a pile of fresh mint, chopped finely, and lamb was roasting in the oven; it was a fusion of smells quite new to me, and mouth-watering. Joseph gave me a light, crispy little pastry; sticky with honey, it had a slightly scented taste. That was the moment, I have always felt, in the distant aromatic kitchen, which awoke my taste buds and kindled my lifelong passion for food and flavour. Many years later the memory of Joseph's dishes and the spices he used were my inspiration when I started to cook and experiment with dishes of my own.

The next morning my mother took me to the souk. I held her hand tightly as we walked out of the bright sun into the dim light of what seemed like an endless arched corridor, with smaller alleys off it, full of mysterious sounds and bustle. People streamed towards us and

Damascus garden salad

The gardener grew salad leaves and a few vegetables near his mud house at the end of the garden and my stepfather asked him to pick the leaves when they were still almost seedlings. Every salad included mint, which is very refreshing during hot weather. In addition, we used to pick a few scented pink rose petals to throw into the salad, as my mother said they looked so pretty amongst the green.

Serves 4

2 Little Gem lettuces

2 handfuls of lamb's lettuce

4 spring onions

bunch of radishes

handful of mint leaves

handful of flat-leafed parsley

few scented rose petals (optional)

30g pine kernels

1 small clove garlic

juice of 1 small lemon

5 tablespoons extra virgin olive oil

sea salt, black pepper

Pull the Little Gem lettuces apart, discarding any marked outer leaves, and put the leaves into a salad bowl. Throw in the lamb's lettuce.

Top and tail the spring onions and radishes and slice both very thinly. Chop the mint leaves and parsley finely. Add the spring onions, radishes and herbs to the lettuce, together with the rose petals if using, and toss to mix.

Put a dry frying pan over a fairly high heat, add the pine kernels and toss around just until browned; transfer to a cold plate and put to one side.

Peel and slice the garlic. Using a pestle and mortar, pound the garlic with 2 level teaspoons sea salt to a smooth purée. Stir in the lemon juice and olive oil and then season with black pepper.

Just before serving, throw the toasted pine kernels into the salad and toss with the olive oil and lemon dressing.

Bloudan walnut soup

Serves 6

1 large white onion

2 tablespoons olive oil

25g butter

2 rounded teaspoons coriander seeds, ground with a pestle and mortar

125g walnut halves or pieces

1 level tablespoon caster sugar

25g plain flour

600ml good chicken stock

750ml whole milk

1 rounded teaspoon cumin seeds

handful of flat-leafed parsley, chopped

handful of mint leaves, chopped

6 tablespoons whole milk yogurt

sea salt, black pepper

A memory of a mildly spiced creamy soup inspired this recipe. The walnuts from our garden at Bloudan were deliciously moist and milky because we ate them fresh. I have since found that if you put walnuts in a bowl, pour boiling water over them and soak them overnight you can restore a bit of the freshness I remember, so do this if you have time.

Peel the onion, cut in half and slice as thinly as you can. Heat the olive oil and butter in a large, heavy-based saucepan over a medium heat until the butter is melted. Add the onion and ground coriander and cook, stirring frequently, for about 10 minutes until the onion is soft and slightly browned. Meanwhile put the walnut pieces into a food processor and pulse to grind finely – don't over-process or the nuts may stick together and become oily.

When the onion is soft, remove the pan from the heat and stir in the sugar and ground walnuts. Then stir in the flour, using a wooden spoon. Gradually stir in the chicken stock and milk, then add the cumin seeds.

Put the saucepan back over a higher heat and bring the soup to the boil, stirring frequently until it bubbles, then cook, stirring, for 2–3 minutes. Now reduce the heat, cover the pan and let simmer very gently for 20 minutes. Season the soup to taste with sea salt and black pepper.

Before serving, stir in the chopped parsley and mint leaves. Ladle the hot soup into individual bowls and add a dollop of yogurt to each.

past us: veiled women with large baskets, traders pushing carts of goods, Bedouin tribesmen carrying camel bridles and harnesses, and little barefoot children. At that time the souk retained much of the exotic character it must have had a hundred years before. Opulent gold brocades shimmered in the half light, printed cottons and delicate vegetable-dyed silks had not yet been replaced by man-made fabrics in garish colours, there were no plastic objects, and almost no Western products. Only the corrugated iron roof, which was held down by stones and punctured by bullet holes, dated from a more recent era when, in 1945, the French bombed Damascus and the souk was machine-gunned from the air. The jagged holes in the roof created thin shafts of sunlight, intensely bright in the darkness; like laser beams they looked as if they would pierce the ground and burn it.

There were restaurants in the souk too. Outside one a young boy with part of a sturdy branch from an olive tree was crushing some raw meat with onion and ground spices into a paste, which my mother told me would be made into long meatballs or sausages, called *kofte*. Having been excited by the smell of freshly ground spices in Joseph's kitchen the day before, I was electrified when we entered the large area of the souk devoted to spices. I found it hard to believe that the vast bowls of many coloured powders, seeds, pieces of bark, piles of pink rose petals and dried leaves could really be used in food. But their heady scents wafted up into the hot air and captivated me. Very soon, thanks to Joseph's skills in the kitchen, I was converted to the kind of dishes that few little English children would have been prepared to accept.

Damascus in 1950 still looked like a place of great antiquity and it had an atmosphere of Arabian Nights. When you saw the elegant minarets of the mosques, the trickling fountains, the mosaic floors and graceful arches of the courtyards within old houses – and the flawlessly clear night sky of the desert, like a dome of midnight-blue enamel decorated with a silver crescent moon and twinkling stars – it was as if you were in a storybook world. Even as such a young child I realised that the city I had come to live in had beauty, drama, danger and mystery, even better than anything I had read about. It has been said that once you have lived in Damascus it lives in you, and I can feel it still.

Playing with our dog Eustace and my stepsister Fidelity.

My bedroom was on the ground floor on one side of the house, and just outside was a fountain surrounded by a small circular pool. I used to sit in the pool on hot days; the cool water just reached my shoulders and the fountain spattered over me. On the other side of the garden wall in the street below I could hear the clip-clop of horses' hooves, occasionally the rumble of a car, and the chatter of the beggar family whose permanent patch was outside our gates. The wide leaves of a large mulberry tree partly shaded the pool, and in late summer the fruit dropped into the water and turned it a clear boiled-sweet dark red. The marmiton would gather the juice-bursting fruit from the tree or the ground and make wonderfully intense 'black mulberry juice', for which Syria is well known.

Bill, my stepfather, loved organising picnics. To the surprise of the British community in Damascus, he had a Nazi car. It was a great whale of a machine called a Horsch that he had noticed in the backyard of the British Embassy in Paris after the Second World War. The car, which was in a derelict state and pockmarked by bullets, had belonged to a Nazi Gauleiter, who may well have been shot at the wheel before the British seized it when the German occupation ended. Bill, who became known as a particularly eccentric diplomat, asked if it was for sale and got it for a knock-down price. It was in this open car that he used to drive us, wearing our white cotton motoring helmets, out to distant rocky outcrops in the Syrian desert, up into the mountains, or to cedar woods near the Lebanese border, taking picnics prepared by Joseph.

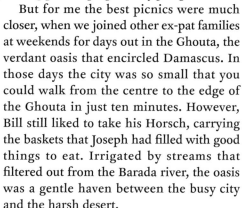

But for me the best picnics were much closer, when we joined other ex-pat families at weekends for days out in the Ghouta, the verdant oasis that encircled Damascus. In those days the city was so small that you could walk from the centre to the edge of the Ghouta in just ten minutes. However, Bill still liked to take his Horsch, carrying the baskets that Joseph had filled with good things to eat. Irrigated by streams that filtered out from the Barada river, the oasis was a gentle haven between the busy city and the harsh desert.

There were almonds, walnuts, olives, pomegranates, vines climbing through the poplars, and all kinds of fruit trees. Above all there were apricots. Linking the orchards were little paths bordered by cyclamen, hyacinths and wild anemones. In a land with a history of conflict that continued to be turbulent, the Ghouta was an idyll of peace. Not surprisingly, it had inspired countless poets and writers over the centuries.

Joseph's lamb flan

We often took this dish, which my mother called a 'flan', on picnics, because we could eat it in our hands. Made with pounded lamb and cracked wheat, it is really a type of *kibbe*, but with added pine kernels. You can serve it warm or at room temperature, with a blob of yogurt.

Serves 6

175g bulghur (cracked wheat)

1 medium onion

500g lean, finely minced lamb

2 rounded teaspoons ground cinnamon

1 medium egg, whisked

35g pine kernels

sea salt, black pepper

Heat the oven to 180°C/Gas 4. Put the bulghur into a bowl of cold water and soak for about 30 minutes, changing the water once, then drain and squeeze dry. Peel and quarter the onion, then put it into a food processor and whiz until finely chopped. Add the bulghur, minced lamb, cinnamon and whisked egg. Season generously with sea salt and plenty of black pepper and whiz very thoroughly until you have a fine paste.

Turn the meat and bulghur mixture into a 25cm earthenware dish and press down evenly with your fingertips. Scatter the pine nuts all over the surface and press them slightly into the mixture with the flat of your hand. Put the dish on a shelf towards the top of the oven and bake for 35–45 minutes until well browned on top. When ready to serve, cut into slices, like a flan.

View from the roof of our house in Damascus in 1950, showing part of the oasis and desert hills.

On our picnic outings Bill was, as ever, a dominant figure. He led the other fathers in energetic ball games, and after lunch could often be seen under an olive tree playing his nose flute or telling stories, as if for the first time. My mother never ceased to roar with laughter at these stories, although we had heard them hundreds of times before. I made friends with the Savage children, Mary-Joy, Brabby and little Georgy, whose father was head of the British Council. We climbed trees, played hide-and-seek with the other children, picked flowers, ate fruit and nuts, and when it was too hot, swam in the cold water of the river. Sometimes we found tortoises, and those of us with gardens took them home. Once I discovered a chameleon, which seemed to me much more exotic, although it moved even less than a tortoise. It sat for months catching flies on the curtains of the room where I had lessons with my governess, turning to a mottled colour that exactly matched the floral pattern. Then one morning my pet chameleon wasn't there, and we never found him.

At the end of our days in the Ghouta, when the sun began to set on the orchards, we would pack up the picnic things and say goodbye to the other families, using the local saying, '*Bukra til Mish-Mish*', or 'See you tomorrow under the apricots'. The taste of those Syrian apricots has remained a most vivid food memory, and the intensity of the ones Joseph used to dry in the sun on the flat roof outside our kitchen made me a dried apricot addict for life. From time to time a Syrian food shop near where I live now in London gets some of the little green figs that I remember – pale pink inside, soft and honey-sweet – but never those perfect apricots of the Ghouta, which must be eaten straight from the tree, still warm from the sun that has nurtured them.

***

Shortly before Bill's children, my older stepbrother and stepsister, were due to come out to Syria from England for their summer holiday, Bill heard that a large stone house in the cooler mountains above Damascus still belonged to the British. Just outside the village of Bloudan, it had been acquired in the early nineteenth century as a cooler refuge for British consuls and their families during the hottest summer months. The last consul to live in it properly had been the legendary adventurer and Arabist Richard Burton and his wife Isabel, at the start of the 1870s. The house was in an advanced state of disrepair, had no electricity and was almost unfurnished, but there was a large garden with a stream running through it, a few walnut trees and spectacular views over six mountain ranges. Bill was determined that we could live in it; he pointed out that there was even a sun-parched croquet lawn.

Inside was some old wooden furniture and rusty iron bedsteads. A quick makeover was done. The walls of the rooms, on which almost all of the original wallpaper had rotted away, were whitewashed, new mattresses and bedding were acquired for the creaky beds, and Barbara had simple curtains made, using cotton from the souk with a pretty design of tiny Damask roses. A few old rugs were found for the stone floors. Although we did not have comforts such as upholstered sofas and armchairs, or hot water, we were still looked after in diplomatic style as our cook Joseph, and Olga, one of the Legation maids, came up from Damascus with us. From two gas rings and an old oven fuelled by olive wood, Joseph produced, as ever, excellent meals.

The stream at the end of the garden was full of frogs and at night there was always a loud frog chorus. The frogs gave Bill an idea. Both he and my mother loved eating frog's legs in France but we children had never heard of such a thing; to us it sounded quite barbaric. Bill insisted that they were a great delicacy and tasted just like chicken. So, when some friends came for a weekend, he proposed a frog hunt. Bill had been told that if he attached a piece of red flannel to a string it would attract the frogs and he would be able to catch them – a sort of red rag to a frog. However, this didn't work and a more elaborate scheme followed. Bill dug out holes in the mud wall on the other side of the stream, chased the frogs into these, then put in his hand and pulled the struggling creatures out, flinging them into a sack. He clearly found it great fun and didn't mind being covered in mud.

Rose petal tart

It was in Syria that I first experienced the romantic pleasure of eating rose petals, which have a tantalising texture and a subtle flavour that is not simply scented. I still buy rose petal jam whenever I can – it is particularly good stirred into yogurt. The filling for the tart is rather like a very light rose-flavoured cheesecake, with delicately crisp petals on top. It is a lovely party piece and a good talking point.

Serves 6–8

For the crystallised rose petals:

petals of 1–2 scented red roses

1 large egg white (yolk reserved for tart filling)

caster sugar for coating

For the short pastry:

200g plain flour

160g cold unsalted butter, cubed

pinch of salt

5–6 tablespoons ice-cold water

For the filling:

300ml double cream

1 large egg yolk

2 level tablespoons caster sugar

125g whole milk yogurt

2 tablespoons rose water

petals of 1 small scented red or pink rose

Crystallise the rose petals in advance – a day or two if you like. Whisk the egg white in a bowl until stiff. Put some caster sugar into another bowl. Lay a piece of non-stick baking parchment on a large baking sheet and turn on the oven to its lowest setting. Dip each rose petal first into the egg white and then into the caster sugar, laying them on the baking sheet as you do so. Place on the lowest shelf of the oven for 1–1½ hours or until the petals are dry and crisp. Ease each one off the parchment very carefully with your thinnest spatula; some will probably crumble but can still be used. Keep the crystallised petals in an airtight container until ready to use.

Make the pastry following the method on page 76. Wrap in cling film and rest in the fridge for about an hour before using.

To make the tart, heat the oven to 200°C/Gas 6 and butter a loose-based 24cm flan tin. Roll out the pastry to a circle, a bit bigger than the flan tin, and use to line the tin, bringing up the edges a bit above the rim – don't try to make them too neat and even. Lightly prick the pastry all over with a fork, then line with foil and weight down with dried beans or rice.

Bake the pastry case on the middle shelf of the oven for 15 minutes. Remove from the oven and lift out the foil with the beans. Lower the oven setting to 160°C/Gas 3.

For the filling, in a large bowl, whip the cream until it is thick but not stiff. Whisk in the egg yolk, sugar and yogurt thoroughly. Gradually whisk in the rose water and then stir in the fresh rose petals. Pour the mixture into the pastry case and bake in the centre of the oven for 20 minutes.

Remove from the oven and leave until cool, then carefully push up the base to lift the tart from the tin. Using a spatula, gently ease the tart onto a serving plate, or you can keep it on the tin base if you feel it is too fragile to transfer. Chill in the fridge to set the filling further.

About an hour before serving, take the tart out of the fridge. At the last moment, sprinkle the top all over with crystallised rose petals. Use a very sharp knife to slice the tart – the filling will still ooze a bit, deliciously.

It was poor Joseph who had the job of cutting the live frogs in half and cooking them. That evening, despite protestations, my stepsister Fidelity and I ate frog's legs and could not deny that they were tender, mild and succulent. Seven of us consumed the legs of over fifty frogs, though it was Bill, as usual, who ate more than anyone else. Early in my childhood Bill noticed that I was almost as greedy as he was and he would watch closely at meals as I spooned food onto my plate, seemingly concerned that there might not be enough for him. Again and again he would say emphatically, using his nickname for me: 'Go slow, Joso'. Even today I feel irritated at the memory.

The mountain air of Bloudan was wonderfully clear and the daytime sky a perfect, deep blue that made it appear impenetrable. In a holiday diary of his first visit Hubert, my stepbrother, wrote after two weeks: 'I saw two tiny clouds today'. When we needed to cool off we rode on donkeys up the track behind the house to the 'swimming pool' of a local doctor, Dr Kahil. In fact the pool was a fairly small but deep stone reservoir with dark, very cold water. It was shaded by a large fig tree laden with small, light green figs that seemed to me like soft little bags full of pink honey and crunchy seeds. One of the branches hung so far over the water that we used to pick the ripe figs while we swam and ate them in the water; I remember even at that age thinking this was a blissful experience.

***

Very soon our garden in Damascus became full of cats. Apart from Bill's prize Siamese cat Dudley, and Eustace, a Maltese terrier, who had both come from England, Fidelity and I collected other cats of all kinds to save them from starvation, as the Syrians hated cats. Every day we gave them a communal meal on the terrace, to which they ran from all corners of the garden. In the end we had nineteen cats who lived happily with Dudley, Eustace, the white doves and even a goat, who shared the gardener's two-room mud house at the end of the garden with him, his wife and their five children. Despite all the animals the garden looked beautiful. In the run up to Christmas a turkey also appeared, to be fattened up for the great day, when Joseph presented it stuffed with spiced cracked wheat, pine kernels and a few of his dried apricots.

It was an idyllic life for a child and the fact that gunfire could often be heard at dawn didn't bother me, nor even the occasion when one of our night guards shot the other dead by mistake. When my mother had my half-brother Matthew at the Victoria Hospital, a missionary hospital near our house that had survived decades of political changes and bombings, the servants rejoiced that it was a boy and I was happy not to be the youngest any more. But the idyll was not to last. Bill and Barbara did not know what to do about my education. The first governess had to leave because of alcoholism and her highly eccentric replacement, who dressed up as a priest every morning and conducted a service to me – her congregation of one – before lessons, soon followed. So they decided to send me back to school in England.

My mother (pictured right with me) was now pregnant again and it was only later that I heard what happened. Barbara was eight months pregnant and she and Bill were giving a large dinner party. As a chocolate soufflé was brought in by Khalil, my mother realised she was bleeding but waited until Bill was leading the guests out of the room at the end of the meal before she told the wife of the Information Officer, who she knew was a nurse. By this time Barbara's chair was scarlet with blood. Although the nursing care at the Victoria Hospital was without fault, the facilities were primitive. Barbara had lost a large amount of blood and needed a Caesarian. There was no plasma for giving her a blood transfusion, and the only anesthetic was a cloth soaked in chloroform that she had to inhale. The operating table was non-adjustable, like a trestle table. But the baby, a girl, cried strongly and everyone was hopeful.

The next day Barbara, who had almost died from loss of blood, tried to feed her tiny baby with drops of milk from a fountain pen, but the tiny girl seemed unable to swallow. Towards the evening she died in my mother's arms. This was the moment, she told me in old age, which she could never forget, when the warmth left the little body so quickly.

The following day Bill was seen carrying a small white coffin from the hospital and putting it on the seat of the Legation car. The two-day-old baby was buried in the Protestant cemetery just outside the ancient walls of Damascus, amongst many sad graves of young children of missionary families, and near to the impressive tomb of Lady Jane Digby, who after many adventurous travels and love affairs, settled in Damascus in 1853 and married a Bedouin Sheikh.

As I was eating my breakfast in the stone-flagged dining room at my new school in Dorset the post was handed round. I was always excited to see a letter from my mother, which she illustrated with crayon drawings of roses and other flowers in the Damascus garden. But this time there were no drawings, just a brief note: 'I'm afraid I have very sad news. My baby was born too soon. She was a sweet little girl but she wasn't strong enough.' My mother never got over the loss of her baby and in old age, with her mind failing, she would ask me to go to the kitchen to 'fetch the baby'.

Apricot and pomegranate jelly

In the Ghouta, during the spring, my favourites – apricots and pomegranates – flowered at the same time, growing side by side like friends. Later, as their fruit ripened, the apricot trees looked as if they might collapse under the weight of the fruit. No shop-bought apricots can bring you the heaven of tree-ripened fruit, still warm from the sun that has brought it to a state of perfection. However, the real taste of apricots is not unattainable; something miraculous can happen when you cook them in the right way. Always choose the darkest apricots you can find, preferably ones with a pink blush.

Joseph made fruit jellies for me because he knew children loved them, but in fact adults are just as enthusiastic. I like to serve jelly with good cream that slides sensually over. People sigh with pleasure.

Serves 6–8

750g apricots

100g golden caster sugar

400ml pure unsweetened pomegranate juice

juice of 2 lemons, strained

6 sheets leaf gelatine

100ml cold water

1 pomegranate

Cut the apricots in half and remove the stones. Put them into a saucepan with the sugar, pomegranate juice and lemon juice and bring to the boil, then simmer gently for about 10 minutes until the fruit is just soft, not mushy. Meanwhile, cut the gelatine into small pieces, put into a heatproof bowl with the cold water and leave to soak.

When the apricots are ready, remove the pan from the heat. Now put the bowl of soaked gelatine over a saucepan of very gently simmering water and stir just until smoothly melted. Pour into the fruit mixture, stirring with a wooden spoon to mix in evenly.

Cut open the pomegranate and scrape the seeds and juice into the fruit mixture, reserving a few seeds for decoration. Stir to mix evenly. Turn into a 1.2–1.3 litre jelly mould or pudding bowl and leave to cool – I find that metal jelly moulds are the most successful for turning out jellies. When cold, chill for several hours, or overnight, until well set.

Before serving, dip the mould briefly in a sink of hot water, then loosen the edges of the jelly with your fingertips and turn out onto a serving plate. If the jelly doesn't plop out easily, a good shake against the plate should do the trick. Scatter the reserved pomegranate seeds on top and refrigerate again until ready to serve.

In Granny's kitchen

y maternal grandmother Enid had the palest, clearest blue eyes imaginable. They sometimes looked sad, but whenever she saw me they filled with pleasure and warmth. I only remember Granny with pure white hair, but paintings of her when she was young by her husband, Percy Jowett, a prolific artist and principal of the Royal College of Art, reveal her thick dark brown hair, which made her eyes look even more incredible. Enid, who came from a family of artists and musicians, had met Percy when they were both art students. They married and remained devoted to each other, but Percy died of a heart attack shortly after I came back from Damascus to live with Granny in London and attend boarding school in the country. It was probably Enid's loss of Percy and mine of my mother who was so far away that made us need and love each other so much. In many valuable ways Granny became my mother.

Granny, like her mother and daughter, was a good and not too plain cook. Seemingly cooking skills run in families but I am not sure if they are hereditary or simply due to enthusiasm passed down through the generations. Whatever the case, an awareness of flavour and the ability to make things taste special must surely be inherited and these are key to good cooking. Granny's kitchen, in the semi-basement of her terrace house in Chelsea, was old fashioned and comforting. In the centre of

the room a pine table looked almost carved by years of scrubbing, and beyond it against the far wall was a mottled grey enamel New World gas cooker with two ovens and cabriolet-shaped legs. On the opposite wall, in front of the stairs, was a dresser arranged with peasant-style French china brought back from summers spent with an artist's colony in France; artist designed mugs hung on hooks. On the top was an ancient preserving jar filled with boiled eggs preserved in isinglass, flanked by two large white Staffordshire dogs, which are the kings of my kitchen dresser today.

A comfy but collapsing armchair in one corner was where I often curled up as I watched Granny cook, and double doors led out onto the small garden. Granny and I spent most of our time in the kitchen. The pine table was even used as an operating table when I had my tonsils out, followed of course by days of eating ice cream.

Next to the kitchen on the street side of the house was a full-sized front room known as 'the boiler room', but also used as a store-room. It smelt of hot coal and the dust of ages, and had shelves crammed with papers, stacks of my grandfather's canvases on the floor and, hanging

Chicken roasted in yogurt and spices

I had got used to things cooked with spices and yogurt in Damascus so I was interested in the few little jars of spices on Granny's shelf, and she always had yogurt for our breakfast. There were caraway seeds that she added to cabbage and cakes, cinnamon for puddings, and cayenne pepper for cheesy things, so one day I persuaded her to try them with my favourite meal – roast chicken.

Serves 4-6

1.6–2kg free-range chicken

juice of 1 lemon

4–5 rounded tablespoons whole milk yogurt

2 rounded teaspoons ground cinnamon

2 level teaspoons caraway seeds

1 level teaspoon cayenne pepper

sea salt

butter for greasing

Make deep cuts in the breast and legs of the chicken and smear with the lemon juice so that it trickles down into the cuts. Leave for half an hour or so at room temperature.

Heat the oven to 180°C/Gas 4. Put the yogurt into a small bowl and mix in the ground cinnamon, whole caraway seeds, cayenne pepper and a good seasoning of sea salt.

Place the chicken in a buttered roasting pan and smear all over and down into the cuts with the spiced yogurt. Roast on the centre shelf of the oven for 1½–1¾ hours, covering the top lightly with a piece of foil if it is getting too brown.

crookedly on one wall, a reproduction of the painting Whistler did of his mother. I used to creep in when Granny was upstairs to see what I could find. By the dim light of one overhead bulb I secretly read my grandparents' love-letters. One day I found a maid's report for the police about finding my father in bed with a woman in a Brighton hotel, which I couldn't comprehend. Years later I was told that the shy, gentle man, whom my mother had left for my stepfather, had to hire a woman to be found with to provide evidence for the divorce.

At that time, my father, Tom, had not yet re-married; he lived alone in one room on Kensington Church Street where I was not allowed to go as it was thought to be 'unsuitable' for a child. He was a quietly charming and humorous eccentric, an architect whose great passions in life were fireworks, jazz and magic. During the war he elected to work with the London Fire Service and enjoyed being surrounded by flames and explosions. Much later, when he re-married and went to live in the country, he began totally illegal experiments, making fireworks himself in his 'den', which resulted in a unique yearly show for his friends and family.

Cheesy fish cakes with spring onions

Granny's fish cakes marked the start of a lifelong passion for me. Granny often made the more usual kind with salmon – usually tinned Canadian – and potato, but sometimes she produced these, which are delicious and lighter as they do not include potato.

Serves 4

350g naturally smoked cod or haddock fillet, skinned

75g fresh white breadcrumbs

bunch of spring onions

100g mature Cheddar cheese, grated

1 teaspoon small capers

½–1 level teaspoon cayenne pepper

1 large egg, plus 1 egg yolk

plain flour for dusting

generous knob of butter

sea salt

Check the fish fillets for any small bones, then chop them up as finely as you can and put into a bowl with the breadcrumbs. Trim and finely slice the spring onions across, using as much of the green part as possible, then add to the bowl with the grated cheese, capers, cayenne pepper and a sprinkling of salt. Mix all together thoroughly with a wooden spoon.

In a small bowl, whisk the whole egg and egg yolk to combine and then stir into the fish mixture. With well-floured hands, take up small handfuls of the mixture and shape into fairly small fish cakes.

Heat the butter in a large frying pan over a medium heat. You will probably have to cook the fish cakes in two batches. Fry them for 5–8 minutes on each side until golden brown, turning carefully with a spatula once only. Transfer to a heated dish. (If necessary you can keep the fish cakes warm in a low oven for up to half an hour.) Serve with good mayonnaise or aïoli, or even a good ketchup.

Enid, who never liked my stepfather Bill, loved cooking for Tom whenever he visited me and, living alone, he was clearly delighted to eat Granny's wonderful food. When she cooked chicken or roast lamb, Tom, who was good at carving, would sharpen the knife rhythmically as if he was the percussion in a jazz band. And because Granny knew Tom loved cheese she often made him cheesy fish cakes, or a savoury custard with three different cheeses. There would always be an irresistible English nursery pudding, such as Granny's mouth-watering Lemon pudding 'delicious', a light and tangy finale that I hope will live on in my family for many more generations. After the meal Tom and I would give magic shows for Granny; Tom's shyness disappeared when he performed and between our tricks he would play his ukulele or the piano and sing.

Granny was the first to make me aware of so-called 'health foods'. Once a week we visited what must have been one of London's first 'health food' shops, in Sydney Street. Here Granny bought her sticky dark brown raw sugar, brown rice, Bemax wheat germ, tall red tins of the twiggy fruit and nut cereal Fru-Grains, intensely flavoured dried apricots, and dried bananas – which I usually ate on the way home.

I had first tasted yogurt in Syria, and was pleased to find that in London Granny had it delivered daily by the milkman in small jars. Rich, glossy brown heather honey with a slight citrus taste was sent regularly from Scotland in green tins. And I became almost addicted to watercress, which Granny plied me with as the doctor said that I was anaemic. But luckily for me Granny was not obsessive about healthy eating. She made rusks from stale bread for me to spread with lumps of beef dripping and lots of the salty dark sediment at the bottom. And she often prepared a meal I craved – roast chicken and 'Potato Puffles', a frozen product, followed by her indulgent rice pudding made with brown rice, dark raw sugar from Barbados and Jersey cream, cooked slowly until richly caramelised, with a dark skin on top.

I went shopping with Granny every morning. The butcher's shop on Old Brompton Road had pale sawdust on the floor and the butcher, with his round, rosy face and large stomach under blood-spattered overalls, was just what I thought an English butcher should be. He loved children and would often give Granny a marrowbone, as I had told him how I loved scooping out and eating the rich, softly set marrow. The greengrocer had a narrow little shop on the corner of Gloucester Road and Old Brompton Road. He was a tall thin man who had lost a leg in the war and limped about very quickly on a wooden one. He told me how satisfying it was now that he could sell bananas

Three cheese custard

Granny made this whenever a friend in the country had given her some freshly laid eggs. Together with warm seedy brown bread and a watercress salad, I thought it was a perfect meal.

Serves 4

For the custard:

4 large free-range eggs

600ml whole milk

50g mature Cheddar cheese, grated

about ¼ nutmeg

2 rounded teaspoons wholegrain mustard

sea salt, black pepper

For the sauce:

50g unsalted butter, plus extra for greasing dish

25g plain flour

300ml whole milk

75g Gruyère cheese, grated

1 free-range egg yolk

about 3 pinches of cayenne pepper

handful of chives

50g Parmesan cheese

Turn the oven on to 150°C/Gas 2. Half-fill a roasting pan with water and place on the middle shelf of the oven to warm up. Butter a 1.2 litre ovenproof round dish.

For the custard, lightly whisk the eggs in a large bowl. Heat the milk in a pan to just below the boil, add the cheese and stir until smoothly melted in, then slowly whisk into the eggs. Grate the nutmeg onto the mixture and stir in, along with the mustard and a good seasoning of sea salt and black pepper. Pour into the prepared dish.

Stand the dish in the roasting pan of warm water in the oven. Bake for 1¼–1½ hours or until the custard feels set when lightly touched in the centre; if the top begins to brown during cooking, cover loosely with foil.

Meanwhile, make the sauce. Melt the butter in a saucepan over a low heat, then, off the heat, stir in the flour. Gradually stir in the milk, then return to the heat and bring to the boil, stirring. Lower the heat and simmer for 2–3 minutes, stirring. Remove from the heat and stir in the grated Gruyère. Once melted, stir in the egg yolk thoroughly. Season with cayenne pepper to taste, and salt if needed. Snip the chives finely into the pan and stir in.

When the custard is ready, heat the grill. Pour the sauce slowly over the custard and finely grate the Parmesan over the top. Briefly put the dish under the hot grill until speckled brown. Serve as soon as you can.

Lemon pudding 'delicious'

Light, tangy and mouth-watering, this is lovely hot or cold – with or without cream. A bowl of strawberries or raspberries on the side is delectable if you're serving it cold. Granny was given the recipe by an American friend and wrote it down in her kitchen notebook, under 'Lemon Pudding (delicious)', hence its title, which adheres to this day.

Serves 6

50g unsalted butter (at room temperature), plus extra for greasing

225g golden caster sugar

finely grated rind and juice of 2 large lemons

4 large free-range eggs, separated

50g self-raising flour

225ml whole milk

½ level teaspoon cream of tartar

icing sugar for sprinkling (optional)

Turn on the oven to 180°C/Gas 4 and place a roasting pan half-filled with water on the centre shelf to warm up. Butter a 1.5–1.75 litre soufflé or other ovenproof dish.

Whisk the butter in a large bowl until soft, then add the sugar and whisk until fluffy. Gradually whisk in the lemon juice, followed by the grated lemon rind and egg yolks. Sift the flour onto the mixture and stir it in with a metal spoon, then gradually stir in the milk. Whisk thoroughly until very smooth.

In a clean bowl, whisk the egg whites with the cream of tartar until they stand in soft peaks. Then, using a metal spoon, fold gently into the pudding mixture, about a quarter at a time. Pour the mixture into the soufflé dish and stand the dish in the roasting pan of water in the oven. Bake for 40 minutes, or slightly less in a fan oven, until risen and golden brown on top. Serve hot or cold, with a little icing sugar sifted over the surface if you like.

and other exotic fruits that people had been deprived of during the war years. His shop, which was always packed, was like a bookshop, with vegetables and fruit on each side piled on shelves right up to the ceiling and spilling way out onto the pavement. A shopping treat was to go to the palatial food hall in Harrods. We always sat down for a rest in the newly opened 'Health Juice Bar' with its previously unheard of combinations of fresh fruit, though I would unfailingly choose their Creamy Banana Whisk, while Granny had simple carrot juice.

I was cherished by Granny and felt very happy living with her, but my first term at boarding school loomed. One evening Granny showed me an old photograph of my mother aged three – one of several Percy had taken of his wife, his beloved only daughter and himself, to take with him to the front in July 1917 for the final year of the war. It was a perfect image of a ravishing little girl with thick golden curls and large thoughtful eyes, but the print had a bullet hole in the middle of it. Granny explained that the photographs were packed with Percy's other belongings in a trench in France, but during the chaos of a battle they were lost. Two years later, after the war ended, the German authorities

Goddess of puddings

Granny introduced me to the justly famous old English classic, Queen of puddings, but one day when we had run out of jam, she tried it with Seville orange marmalade instead. It was so good that when I reproduced it as a recipe some years later – adding a hint of cardamom – I elevated the queen to a goddess. You can serve the pudding either hot or cold, with or without cream.

Serves 6

75g fresh white breadcrumbs

600ml whole milk

finely grated rind and juice of 1 lemon

finely grated rind of 2 oranges

50g unsalted butter, plus extra for greasing

3 large free-range eggs, separated

125g golden caster sugar, plus extra for sprinkling

4 rounded tablespoons Seville orange marmalade

4 cardamom pods

pinch of sea salt

Heat the oven to 180°C/Gas 4. Butter an ovenproof oval dish and scatter the breadcrumbs over the bottom. Pour the milk into a saucepan and add the grated rind of the lemon and one of the oranges. Add the butter and stir over a low heat until it has melted and the mixture is just warm.

In a large bowl, lightly whisk the egg yolks with 75g of the sugar. Slowly stir in the warm milk and butter, then pour the mixture over the breadcrumbs. Bake in the centre of the oven for about 25 minutes or until the custard feels set when you touch it lightly in the middle. Remove from the oven.

Stir the marmalade and lemon juice together in a bowl. Extract the seeds from the cardamom pods, grind them using a pestle and mortar, then stir into the marmalade. Spread the mixture over the top of the baked custard.

In a clean bowl, whisk the egg whites with the salt until they stand in soft peaks. Using a metal spoon, fold in the remaining sugar and orange zest. Pile this meringue over the marmalade and sprinkle a little extra sugar on top. Return the pudding to the oven for 10–15 minutes until golden brown.

returned this photograph to Percy, as luckily it had his name on the back. It had been found in the breast pocket of a dead German soldier who had clearly liked the picture of the pretty little girl and put it in his pocket before being shot through it.

Granny gave me the photograph to take to boarding school and I put it in a camel leather frame my mother had bought for me in the Damascus souk. It sat on my bedside locker beside a picture taken of Granny and me outside Harrods (on page 26). Sadly, sometime later, I lost that historic photograph with a hole, though I retain a duplicate (pictured left). I began to enjoy my newly independent life at school and make close friends, but I always looked forward to being back in the cocoon of Granny's kitchen during the holidays, and to tasting Lemon pudding 'delicious' and her fish cakes once more.

POTATOES in the ANDES

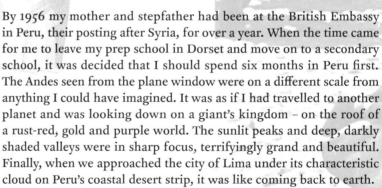

By 1956 my mother and stepfather had been at the British Embassy in Peru, their posting after Syria, for over a year. When the time came for me to leave my prep school in Dorset and move on to a secondary school, it was decided that I should spend six months in Peru first. The Andes seen from the plane window were on a different scale from anything I could have imagined. It was as if I had travelled to another planet and was looking down on a giant's kingdom – on the roof of a rust-red, gold and purple world. The sunlit peaks and deep, darkly shaded valleys were in sharp focus, terrifyingly grand and beautiful. Finally, when we approached the city of Lima under its characteristic cloud on Peru's coastal desert strip, it was like coming back to earth.

My mother and Bill stood on the tarmac as I stumbled out of the plane after my two-day journey. I had not seen my mother for a year and was taken aback by how much thinner she looked. She had always been slim but now had a more sophisticated glamour, like the mannequins in *L'Officiel*, the French fashion magazine, which she followed closely. Only ten years ago I learnt that during their first year in Peru, Barbara had a breakdown and was not seen in public for several months. The tragic death of her baby in Damascus was still

recent and the following depression was, as often at that time, untreated, with the result that even at the end of her life she was still grieving. She had other regrets too. She was torn between supporting Bill, who was clearly the love of her life, and feelings of duty to her children, my half-brother Matthew and me. When my three children were little she wrote to me about the happy family life she had, but added, '... when I look back at my career as a mother, I remember nothing but guilt and shame.'

An ancient chauffeur, Ricardo, drove us into Lima in the embassy Rolls Royce, with its Union Jack flag fluttering on the bonnet, to the residence in Pablo Bermudez. It was a large, imposing house built by the British in 1935 and covered in flowering creepers. Inside the tall iron gates stood Bill's new car, a dashing scarlet Buick Special that replaced his Nazi Horsch. I was introduced to a diverse group of servants (pictured above): Andre, the French cook, with his wife and a cheeky little boy called Thierry; two Peruvian Indian butlers called Kalixto and Benaventura; a warm and smiling maid called Consuela, and her aunt Ludmilla who did the laundry, and a gardener. There was also little Matthew's old-fashioned, neatly uniformed nanny, Miss Toller, who was thin, prim and grey-haired. To me she looked ancient, and she must have been quite old, as her claim to fame was that she had been Peter Ustinov's nanny.

At that moment I heard an English upper class shriek, a long drawn out 'Hello', which was then repeated by a slightly different but still screeching tone of voice. We walked out of the long drawing room onto a covered veranda where there was a parrot in a cage. The bird had clearly listened in on so many cocktail parties that he had learnt

how to greet people with the only word he could distinguish in the party babble. That night, in my bedroom on the street side of the house, I woke up suddenly and thought I heard the parrot shrieking again, but it was human shouts this time. I felt as if I was still on the plane going through a bad patch of turbulence, then realised my room was shaking. I lay without moving as the wardrobe rattled and the fringe on my bedside lamp trembled. It was not until my mother came in and told me not to worry as it was only a tremor that I realised I was experiencing a small earthquake. In the morning it didn't look all that small; out of my window I saw a long deep crack running down the centre of the road.

Andre's cooking was not exceptional but his ingredients were, as a visit to the market showed me. The vegetables, including every kind and colour of chilli, were wonderful, and the fruit was larger than any I'd seen before. There were creamy chirimoyas, or custard apples, moist pink-fleshed bananas, papayas of all sizes, golden physalis fruit from the Andes, flaming-orange persimmons dripping with juice, and most delicious of all, two kinds of passion fruit – large, sweet, scented granadillas, and marguyas, which were sharper with deep orange flesh. Against one wall were the fruit juice vendors (pictured below left); a row of cheerful women almost engulfed by impressive fresh fruit of all kinds, who stood behind their counter, shouting to each other and their customers. First I tried papaya and orange juice, followed boldly by carrot and beetroot with vanilla and a little honey from the jungle.

The fish and shellfish glistened and shone, almost still moving, as if they had been caught minutes before. There were many fish I didn't recognise, alongside familiar sea bass, sole, salmon, crayfish, langoustines and my favourite scallops, with their delectable dark orange coral. One of the fishmongers gave me a little scallop to eat raw, which I did after a brief hesitation. It literally melted in my mouth, like a scallop from heaven. I realised too that Peruvians love talking about food. My mother, who had learnt good Spanish, explained that almost every conversation we overheard was about ways of cooking what was available that day. And this food talk didn't only go on in the market; at any gathering the conversation would frequently turn to food.

Lima was intensely social, and there were often fancy-dress parties to Bill's delight (see page 36). At home, Andre and the servants were kept busy, as the scale of entertaining was extraordinary. One of Bill's letters describes the annual celebrations for the Queen's birthday that took place in the drawing room and garden, with the parrot listening in on the veranda. 'At midday we had the Peruvians and the diplomats – four hundred,' he wrote, and continued, 'and in the evening we had the British Colony – five hundred of them, who fell on the food like vampires, ground their cigarettes into the carpets and drank five dozen bottles of whisky, two dozen of brandy, one dozen of gin and a lot of vermouth and beer.' At a dance held for a naval visit there were 1,600 guests with 'the garden lit up, the band from HMS Superb playing, and sailors doing acrobatic turns'. A fairly small dinner party would be for about thirty people. No wonder my mother had a breakdown.

* * *

I spent a term at the English speaking school in Lima, San Silvestre. The school coat of arms was a British lion flanked by a Peruvian llama and the motto below ran, 'I can, I ought, I will'. I soon developed the so-called 'Lima accent', a sort of half-American half-English sing-song,

Fish with avocado, lime and chilli

I had a similar dish to this for lunch by the sea near Lima and loved the mingling of ingredients. I can't remember what variety of fish was used, but any good-textured white fish will do.

Serves 4

4 thick cod steaks

milk for soaking

225g shallots or small onions

3 large cloves garlic

2 fresh red chillies

500g ripe tomatoes (plum variety if available)

3 tablespoons olive oil

1 level tablespoon tomato purée

grated rind and juice of 2 limes

1 teaspoon caster sugar

1 large avocado

lemon juice for sprinkling

sea salt

Put the fish steaks into a dish in which they fit fairly snugly and pour on enough milk to cover. Cover the dish with cling film and leave in the fridge for at least 2 hours. Lift out the fish and pat dry with kitchen paper. Discard the milk.

Peel the shallots and slice across thinly. Peel the garlic and chop finely. Cut open the chillies under running water, discard the seeds and stem and then slice the chillies across finely.

Pierce the tomatoes, place in a bowl and pour boiling water over them. Leave for a few minutes, then take out, peel and chop finely.

Heat the olive oil in a wide, heavy-based flameproof casserole over a medium heat. Add the shallots and stir for a few minutes until soft and golden. Add the garlic and chillies and stir for another minute.

Now add the chopped tomatoes with their juice, tomato purée, lime rind and juice, sugar and a sprinkling of sea salt. Put the lid on the casserole and bubble gently, stirring now and then, for about 10 minutes until the tomatoes are pulpy and form a thick sauce.

Place the fish steaks on top of the sauce, re-cover and cook over a low heat for 10–15 minutes or until the fish is opaque and feels just about firm when lightly pressed.

Meanwhile, halve the avocado and remove the stone, then carefully peel off the skin. Slice the avocado flesh across thinly into half-moon shapes and sprinkle with lemon juice.

When the fish is cooked, remove the casserole from the heat. Scatter the avocado slices over the fish steaks and serve as soon as possible.

but I disgraced myself by not being able to march in time to the Peruvian National Anthem. *Somos Libres* ('we are free') we trilled as we paced, but I didn't feel free at all in this rather strict, old-fashioned ambience and was relieved when the term ended, my step-siblings Hubert and Fidelity came out for a holiday, and Bill announced that we would go on a journey round Peru in the Buick Special.

At that time there were no asphalt roads in Peru outside the cities, so our red car soon became pale pink with dust and our hair almost white. But it was wonderful to drive out of Lima and escape the cloud that hangs over it for much of the year, shutting out the sun and trapping in the incredibly high humidity. Now we had dry air and clear skies. But also, as we climbed up into the Andes with the bends in the road becoming ever more hairpin and the drop below us steeper and deeper, we had increasing reason to be fearful of Bill's driving. As a young man he had driven over a cliff and almost died, but this had not made him any more cautious and minor crashes punctuated his entire life. My mother sat through every journey in a state of tension, her knuckles white as she gripped the seat, while Bill drove happily and recklessly along.

Our drives between destinations were exceptionally long, as there were very few places to stay; the longest was seventeen hours in one day. Early one morning, on a high barren plain, we stopped in a small village surrounded by eerily dark lakes. Breakfast had been at 5am and I was eager to buy some grilled *choclo*, the local corn-on-the-cob with kernels the size of hazelnuts, which I had spotted on a roadside stall with a charcoal fire alongside. But the stallholder was walking away to join a large crowd – the entire village, it seemed (pictured above) – who were surrounding a man with a crushed foot. The local shaman was attempting to cure him by magic. The shaman looked exactly as I had imagined a witch doctor would. He was wild haired, with a fierce expression and piercing eyes, and wore a long dark robe. In a tin at his feet was a coiled-up snake.

We watched from a distance as Bill pushed his way through the crowd with his camera. When the shaman saw him he shouted angrily, put a poisonous arrow in his large bow and aimed it directly at Bill. There was a tense silence. Bill showed no alarm, but made a stop sign with his hand and said slowly and calmly in English, 'No thank you.'

This was his salvation. The whole crowd, most of whom had never seen foreigners before, burst out laughing, which so disconcerted the shaman that Bill was able to get away and rejoin us. We drove off quickly, though I still longed for the hot smoky *choclo*.

One of the extraordinary things about travelling in Peru is that you can be breathless at an altitude of 16,000 feet one morning and by the evening have driven down to tropical jungle. In a few hours you can descend or climb through several different climates and types of vegetation, so it's no surprise that almost any variety of vegetable or fruit can be grown in Peru. We descended from the high rocky plain with its sombre lakes and the shaman's village into spectacular wooded gorges; from here we could see a silvery river meandering far below. Rhododendrons and fuchsias grew side by side with brilliantly coloured flowering trees and what looked like giant houseplants. We circumnavigated a recent landslide of boulders on the road, narrowly missing some stones that were still tumbling down the mountain. In the late afternoon our surroundings changed even more dramatically. We plunged into dense green jungle where tall rainforest trees, hung with long trails of shiny creepers, tried to reach the distant sky. Bright green parakeets and striking black and yellow birds swooped from one branch to another. Orchids grew on the trunks of the trees and

Top: Women and children in the Urubamba valley.
Above left: Approaching Cuzco, the Inca capital.
Above right: An Inca-built wall in Cuzco.
Right: Machu Picchu.

Peru's national animal, the llama – on the roadside.

we passed gorges with tumbling waterfalls, fringed by creepers and ferns. The shot silk wings of large swallowtail butterflies shimmered blue-green as they flew like birds through slanting shafts of sunlight. A group of Indians with long glossy black hair and geometric fringes, wearing only a piece of cloth round their waists, were taking a carved wooden boat down to a green river. We continued on our way to the Perene valley, where we were to spend a few days staying in a coffee planter's guesthouse and catching exotic butterflies.

It wasn't until we reached the old Inca capital of Cuzco, with its unique mixture of mighty Inca walls and elaborate Spanish colonial buildings, that I discovered what potatoes could be like. Peru is said to be the birthplace of the potato and countless varieties are still grown. There is an image of a potato god from 400AD, holding a potato plant in each hand, and for one hundred years from 1438, the nutritious potato fed the Inca Empire. The quality of what we might think of as the humble potato is something quite different in Peru, like an emerald to a piece of green glass, or like all sorts of different precious stones to fragments of multi-coloured glass. In Cuzco market I saw potatoes of all colours and shapes with textures and tastes that only the high Andes can give. Peruvian potato farmers may well pray to the potato god nowadays, as it is thought that global warming is promoting disease and a necessity to plant the potatoes at higher and higher altitudes. All I know is that the potatoes we ate seemed an unparalleled delicacy.

Machu Picchu, the famous Lost City of the Incas, which is set almost inaccessibly amongst jungle-covered mountains, was not discovered until 1911. Trains crammed with tourists now travel on the dramatic narrow-gauge track from Cuzco to the bottom of the mountain topped by the ruins, but in 1956 we drove through the Urubamba valley to Ollantaytambo station to board a tiny private train, called an Auto Carril. Like a self-propelled carriage, it had nine seats and we shared it with another family, chugging along at about 15mph. We entered a gorge and as it deepened the light became theatrical. It was a dark and mysterious scene with shafts of sunlight piercing through the trees, spotlighting individual tropical flowers, glossy foliage, flashes of little streams and the occasional Inca ruin. Like a Boy's Own adventure story our tiny vehicle became more and more dwarfed by the cone-shaped green mountains all round us.

At the bottom of the Machu Picchu mountain a little bus took us up the narrow road with sixteen S bends, to access the site. At the top, beside the half-excavated city, was a low green hut with a corrugated iron roof where we were to stay the night. From my iron bed I could see the side of the forested sheer mountains on the other side of the Urubamba river, which snaked through the gorge far, far below. Clouds

Peruvian potatoes

There are countless potato recipes in Peru. In Cuzco we had a dish like this as a first course, but it's also good with grilled meat or fish, or with ham. The closest to wonderful Andean potatoes are just-dug, home-grown varieties; for shop-bought I'd recommend Charlotte.

Serves 4–5

1 small red onion

4 tablespoons lemon juice

2 pinches of cayenne pepper

2 fresh green or red chillies

750g small waxy potatoes, such as Charlotte

4 large free-range eggs

2 tablespoons extra virgin olive oil

175g cottage cheese

150ml double cream

1 level teaspoon turmeric

sea salt

Peel the onion and slice as finely as possible into rings. Separate the rings and place in a shallow bowl. Add the lemon juice, cayenne pepper and a little salt. Stir, then cover the bowl and put to one side.

Cut open the chillies under running water, discard the seeds and stem and then chop finely. Wash but don't peel the potatoes and steam or boil until just cooked through. Drain and leave until cool enough to handle.

Meanwhile, boil the eggs for about 7 minutes; the whites should be firm, with the yolks still slightly soft.

At the same time, heat the olive oil in a small pan over a low heat and fry the chopped chillies for 2–3 minutes. Put the cottage cheese, cream, turmeric and a little salt into a food processor. Add the fried chillies along with the oil from the pan and whiz until smooth.

Drain the marinated onion rings. Cut the hot potatoes in half lengthways and arrange in a warmed shallow serving dish. Peel the semi-hard-boiled eggs, halve lengthways and arrange amongst the potatoes. Pour the sauce over the potatoes and eggs, arrange the onion rings on top and serve.

passed immediately in front of me at speed, temporarily obscuring all or part of the mountains, but the next moment they were gone and crystal clear sunlight highlighted flowers I had seen before in very different surroundings: daturas dripping with trumpet-like flowers, giant begonias, day lilies, and scarlet shrubs and creepers with yellow snapdragon-type flowers.

Tiny blue flowers carpeted some of the ruined Inca houses and delicate yellow orchids grew out of cracks between the vast, curved grey stones of the walls. Clambering over a large ruin I found a courgette plant covered with small courgettes, which I picked and munched raw, wondering if it had first been planted in an Inca's kitchen garden. For our supper in the green hut we were given cactus sprouts fried in a light batter; they were delicious and I longed for more. That night I reflected on the Incas' mysterious past life in this isolation, with still unanswered questions about how they manoeuvred those mighty stones to such an inaccessible place. As the old city and mountains became dark around us and the moon flashed between the racing clouds, the atmosphere was almost unearthly, made even more so by our bus driver singing Quechua (the Inca language) songs to a guitar.

* * *

You can never see the opposite shore of Lake Titicaca, the largest lake in South America and, at 13,000 feet, one of the highest in the world. The clarity of light and colour at this altitude, and the huge sky and sculptural clouds sharply reflected in the glassy water, are astonishing. The water is streaked with blue, purple, green, red, yellow and silver, always changing. We stayed in the railway hotel in the shabby town

of Puno, on the shore of the lake. The manager, Signor Bassano, was one of many Italians who came to Puno between the two world wars to trade with Bolivia on the other side of the lake. In this surreal place on the roof of the world, we ate good Italian food washed down with coca leaf tea to ward off altitude sickness. Still today you can get excellent pizzas in Puno.

The manager of the local bank took us out to see some of the floating reed islands on the lake in his smart launch. The islands were created and colonised centuries before by a small pre-Incan tribe, the Uros, when the Incas arrived and took over their land. They built the islands, their houses and boats from the lake's reeds, and fed themselves entirely on fish, birds and a few crops that they could grow among the reeds. Today the Indians are used to tourists and are linked to mainland life by ferries, but only shortly before our visit

Dum's chocolate pudding

Everyone in Lima knew, or knew about Dum Tweedie, and some had been lucky enough to taste his chocolate pudding. It has a featherlight texture with a gooey base, and is rich but not sickly. A treat for chocoholics everywhere, it is equally good hot or cold. Serve with a bowl of crème fraîche.

Serves 6–8

150g dark chocolate (at least 70% cocoa solids)

150g unsalted butter, plus extra for greasing

150ml warm water

2 teaspoons vanilla extract

100g golden caster sugar

4 large free-range eggs, separated

25g plain flour

½ level teaspoon cream of tartar

Turn on the oven to 200°C/Gas 6. Half-fill a roasting pan with water and place on the centre shelf of the oven to warm up. Butter a 1.5–1.75 litre ovenproof dish.

Break the chocolate into small pieces, cut up the butter and put both into a bowl set over a pan of very hot but not boiling water. Stir until melted and smooth. Remove from the heat and gradually stir in the warm water followed by the vanilla extract and sugar.

Pour the chocolate mixture into a large bowl and mix in the egg yolks. Sift the flour onto the chocolate mixture and whisk to combine until free of any lumps. In a clean bowl, whisk the egg whites with the cream of tartar until they stand in soft peaks. Then, using a metal spoon, fold lightly but thoroughly into the chocolate mixture.

Pour the mixture into the prepared dish and stand it in the roasting pan of water in the oven. Bake for 10 minutes, then lower the oven setting to 160°C/Gas 3 and cook for another 30 minutes. If you decide to serve the pudding cold, grate some extra chocolate over the top.

Beef in chilli and chocolate sauce

Several Peruvian savoury dishes include a small amount of chocolate, which enriches the taste and texture. The chocolate used in Peru was far more bitter than any available here, and I find this sauce works best with unsweetened cocoa powder.

Serves 4–5

1 medium onion

2 large cloves garlic

3–4 fresh green or red chillies

75g pecan pieces

25g seedless raisins

4–5 cloves

400g tin tomatoes

1 rounded tablespoon cocoa powder

2 tablespoons sunflower oil

20g butter

1 rounded teaspoon ground cinnamon

600ml beef or vegetable stock

finely grated rind and juice of 1 orange

750g lean stewing steak

bunch of spring onions

sea salt

Peel and roughly chop the onion and garlic. Cut open the chillies under running water, discard the seeds and stem and then chop the chillies roughly. Put these ingredients into a food processor and add the pecans, raisins, cloves, tomatoes and cocoa powder. Whiz thoroughly until as smooth as possible.

Heat 1 tablespoon of the sunflower oil and the butter in a large flameproof casserole over a medium heat. Add the ground cinnamon and stir around once, then add the blended mixture and let it bubble, stirring constantly, for about 5 minutes. Stir in the stock and grated orange rind and juice. Season with a little salt if needed, and remove from the heat.

Heat the oven to 150°C/Gas 2. Cut the beef into cubes; you will need to brown it in batches. Heat the remaining tablespoon of sunflower oil in a large frying pan over a very high heat. Fry the beef cubes quickly, in batches, turning until just browned all over, then add to the casserole along with any pan juices. Stir to combine with the sauce.

Put the casserole back over the heat and bring the sauce to a simmer, then cover and transfer to the oven. Cook for 2½–3 hours until the meat is very tender and the sauce has reduced and thickened.

A minute or so before serving, trim the spring onions and slice across thinly, using as much of the green part as possible, then stir into the casserole.

in 1956 they had, in what was often intense cold, worn no clothes at all. On some islands the Uros were hostile to visitors but the bank manager took us to one where he knew they would be shy but friendly.

Once on the island we had little time to get used to the spongy, sinking sensation with every step we took. On the far side we could see some Uros burning an area to make it more fertile for crops. Suddenly the sky blackened and the wind changed and strengthened. Huge flames spread towards the Uros houses and the reeds looked like gold against clouds of dark smoke. Sparks sprayed upwards like fireworks. The islanders looked unconcerned. Seeing the sparks getting close to his petrol-filled boat, the driver shouted '*Rápido, rápido!*' Getting to the boat quickly was easier said than done; it was like trying to wade through soft mud as our feet sunk into the packed reeds. The driver tried to start the engine but the propeller stuck. Now Uros families were calmly getting into their boats to leave the burning island and head for another, seemingly unmoved by our plight. Finally the engine came to life and, enveloped in smoke, we drew away, leaving an inferno behind us. The island was a huge wall of flame. 'This quite often happens', said the bank manager, unpacking our picnic lunch.

After an extensive journey lasting a month we arrived back in Lima. It was dark when we reached the house in Pablo Bermudez and my mother, to the obvious disapproval of Nanny, fetched five-year-old Matthew from his bedroom. Andre had cooked some tender beef with chilli and chocolate. And our friend Dum Tweedie, a great character in the British community, who had a brother called Dee, had brought his famous chocolate pudding to welcome us back. After dinner, as we told Dum about our adventures, the parrot on the veranda screeched 'Hello, Hello' insistently until Bill went and covered the cage with a cloth.

Chilled passion fruit snow

This is my recreation of one of Andre's mainstays, which everyone loved. Sometimes it's possible to find large passion fruit – similar to the ones we had in Peru – if so, you will only need 4 or 5 of them.

Serves 6–7

3 rounded tablespoons orange blossom or wildflower honey

juice of 2 large lemons

2 level teaspoons powdered gelatine

4 large free-range eggs, separated

6 passion fruit

pinch of salt

Put the honey and lemon juice in a small saucepan and heat gently until the honey has melted. Remove from the heat, sprinkle in the gelatine and stir well until it has dissolved completely; if there are still lumps you can put the pan back over a very low heat but the mixture must not bubble. Set aside.

Put the egg yolks into a heatproof bowl that fits over a saucepan, or use a double boiler if you have one. Add the honey, lemon and gelatine mixture to the egg yolks and mix thoroughly, using a wooden spoon. Half-fill the saucepan with water and bring just to the boil over a high heat, then lower the heat. Set the bowl over the pan (making sure it isn't in direct contact with the water) and stir the mixture constantly for about 5 minutes until thickened slightly. Remove the bowl from the heat.

Place a sieve over the bowl. Cut open 5 passion fruit and, using a sharp teaspoon, scoop out the flesh into the sieve. Rub the flesh in the sieve with a small wooden spoon to extract as much juice as possible – only the seeds should remain. Lift off the sieve (don't throw away the seeds) and stir the sieved passion fruit flesh and juice into the egg yolk mixture. Finally, scoop out the flesh and seeds of the remaining passion fruit into the mixture and stir well. Pour into a larger bowl and leave to cool slightly.

In a clean bowl, whisk the egg whites with the salt until they hold soft peaks. Using a metal spoon, gently but thoroughly fold the whisked egg whites into the passion fruit mixture. Pour into a pretty glass serving bowl or individual bowls. Scatter a few of the sieved passion fruit seeds on top and place in the fridge. The 'snow' will be set in about 2 hours.

THE ISLAND OF VOLCANOES

Doctor's orders took my mother and Bill to Lanzarote. During the winter of 1960 Bill, who was by then posted in Switzerland, had a small heart attack and was told he should go somewhere warm to recuperate. The nearest place was the Canary Islands and Bill, adventurous as ever, chose the one that sounded the most unusual, and where tourism was almost non-existent. There was one hotel on the island, a government-owned *parador* in Arrecife, the main town. By the end of their holiday Bill had fallen in love with the strange island, three-quarters covered in dark cone-shaped volcanoes, old craters and lava flows. On their last day he bought a house in an isolated fishing village, Playa Blanca, at the far south of the island. The village was surrounded by desert hills and reached by an unmade road, which cut through a sea of bronze black lava that looked as if it had bubbled out of a volcano the day before and, still molten, was moving slowly towards the sea. The time it took to get from Arrecife to Playa Blanca on a bad road, and the weird terrain we passed through on the way, made me think of it as the village at the end of the world.

The landscape of Lanzarote was, and still is, quite extraordinary. It was dotted with volcanoes – a number of them still live and hot – of colours ranging from pitch black to purple, red, orange and yellow from the sulphur in the lava. Surrounding the volcanoes were fields covered in powdered black lava to retain moisture. Chickpeas and other crops, neatly planted in protective holes, looked a brilliant emerald green against the black earth, while the fig trees, leafless in winter and each one surrounded by its own little wall to shield it from the wind, appeared to be made of silver.

Ploughs were pulled by camels, which must have been brought over from Africa many hundreds of years before, and the only large trees were occasional palms. There were a few small villages of whitewashed flat-roofed houses with all of their windows and doors painted bright green – a law on the island. But beyond the cultivation and tumbling lava streams, it was the desert hills surrounding our village that reminded me of the golden hills outside Damascus and made me feel very much at home.

Chicken with chickpeas and chorizo

Rather like the eggs they laid, the scrawny chickens who pecked around all over the village tasted good. In this quick and easy dish, their flavour was also enhanced by spicy chorizo and a sprinkling of the hard, slightly salty goat's cheese we got from the lady on the mountain. You can now buy fresh chorizo sausages for cooking here, and these are the best ones to use for this dish.

Serves 5-6

3 large cloves garlic

4 large chicken thighs, boned and skinned

250g fresh chorizo sausages (for cooking)

2 tablespoons sunflower oil

2 x 400g tins chickpeas

400g tin chopped tomatoes

1 tablespoon tomato purée

1 rounded tablespoon dried oregano

50g pitted black olives

100g hard goat's cheese

2 tablespoons extra virgin olive oil

sea salt, black pepper

Peel the garlic and chop roughly. Slice each chicken thigh across into 3 or 4 pieces. Slice the chorizo sausages across into about 4 pieces.

Heat the sunflower oil in a heatproof casserole over a high heat, then add the chicken and chorizo pieces and stir around just to brown slightly. Now stir in the chopped garlic.

Drain the chickpeas and add them to the casserole with the chopped tomatoes, tomato purée, oregano and black olives. Bring up to bubbling point over a high heat, then put the lid on the casserole and turn the heat right down. Cook as gently as possible for 20–30 minutes until the chicken is cooked through.

Grate the goat's cheese and put into a serving bowl. Once the chicken is cooked, season to taste with sea salt and black pepper and trickle the olive oil over the surface.

Serve straight from the casserole, with the grated cheese alongside for people to sprinkle on themselves.

Beyond Playa Blanca there wasn't even a track, but Bill found it was just possible to drive across the pebbly desert to several coves with pristine sandy beaches, unvisited by anyone except the occasional fisherman. After a day of swimming and picnicking on one of the beaches, my mother and Bill came back to the village where Salvador, an enterprising and good-looking fisherman, had just set up a small café on the village beach that had a well in the centre and a roof made of palm tree branches.

Bill asked if there were any houses for sale in the village and was told that an old man who owned two small, flat-roofed cottages on a promontory facing the sea might be persuaded to sell. He lived with a large family of children and grandchildren, seemingly firmly settled, but when Bill offered him £200 for both cottages it was clearly a sum he could never have dreamed of. It was agreed that Bill should come back the next day to arrange the deal, but the excitement was too much for the old man, and that night he died of a heart attack. Nevertheless, when Bill and my mother appeared next morning and found the grieving family, they still agreed to sell the cottages.

The following winter my little half-brother and I visited for the first time, to stay for the Christmas holidays. We flew first to Gran Canaria and then on to Lanzarote in a rickety little Fokker Friendship plane with very few others. By then the two cottages had been joined together to make a simple one-story house, flat roofed and whitewashed like all the others on the island, but with four bedrooms and a large living area all facing the sea and the distant island of Fuerteventura.

We woke in the morning to the sound of the sea just below the house and the crowing of cocks in the village, and I lay drowsily looking at lizards darting across the white walls of the room. The village had no electricity or telephone then, or for the following twenty years. But we had gas lamps to read by and a Calor gas stove to cook on, and even a cook called Maria (pictured above with her family), who became an important part of our life there. Maria was small and very round, almost as wide as she was high, with a wonderful smile. She lived in a derelict house with six young children who she had to support. Her husband, who she said used to tear off her clothes and beat her up, had died when he had fallen from the roof, while full of Spanish brandy, and hit a rock below. Maria couldn't read or write, but with my mother's guidance, she became a very good and experimental cook, making the most of the fresh but limited local ingredients.

Empty beaches with fine pale sand and transparent blue sea were the real treat in the area at that time. Almost every day on these beaches we ate simple but delicious picnics, prepared by Maria. Overhanging rocks provided shade and Bill would lay out the picnic on a tablecloth. We tucked into Spanish omelette and tomato salad, usually followed by a large bowl of strongly scented guavas, peeled and prepared on the beach by Bill. He would always end the meal by dipping a bunch of grapes in the sea as he said, quite rightly, that a touch of salt made them taste extra good.

Something about the fertile volcanic soil and the dry climate of Lanzarote produced wonderful vegetables, particularly tomatoes and small muscatel grapes, and potatoes that could almost rival Peruvian ones. There was very little rainfall on the island and every house had a slope on the roof so they could collect any rain that fell in a big tub underneath. During our first years, with no desalination plant, water was more expensive to buy than the local rough sherry-type wine. We had to be very sparing with water for washing, and flush the loo with saved washing-up water. But the lack of fresh water had some bonuses. Maria used to boil vegetables in sea water and this left a white sea salt crust on the little new potatoes in their skins – the memory of those potatoes with their salty coating, eaten cold with Maria's home-made mayonnaise, makes my mouth water as I write.

The eggs Maria used for her mayonnaise – from chickens that roamed all over the village and on the rocks by the sea, with not a leaf of green to peck at – were miraculously delicious, with deep orange yolks. In a village that didn't have either greenery or rubbish collections, the high quality of the eggs must have been the result of a diet of discarded fish trimmings and people's scraps. I can't remember having roast chicken, the scrawny village chickens were probably too tough, but I do remember Maria's chicken soup. It was thickened with gofio – finely ground toasted maize or chickpeas, said to have originated with the Guanches, the first known inhabitants of the Canary Islands. Rich in vitamins, gofio had been used on Lanzarote for hundreds of years by the islanders, to make a kind of gruel whenever they could not afford or obtain anything else for their large families. It gave a good nutty flavour to Maria's soup.

One year there was a plague of jellyfish, the lethal Portuguese Men of War, which often landed up on the beach, so we had to be careful where we trod and look out for them in the sea. Bill took no notice and swam into caves full of them; he even suggested they could be good to eat. He was not squeamish about food and often talked about his experiences of eating live ants, locusts and other insects. He delighted in telling us that as the guest of honour at a Bedouin encampment in Syria he had happily eaten a raw sheep's eye. Before the war, in Belgrade, Bill's first diplomatic post, he arranged for a regular supply of tortoises from South Serbia, when he was told that they made just as good a soup as turtles.

Chilled almond and garlic soup

Freshly ground almonds make all the difference to the flavour of this Spanish soup, which my mother taught Maria how to make. I recall her pounding almonds laboriously with a stone pestle and mortar, but of course we can use a food processor. When you are able to use mild, sweet, new season's garlic, you won't need to add the sugar.

Serves 6

2 large heads of garlic (as fresh as possible)

1 large Spanish onion

1 litre whole milk

2 rounded teaspoons caster sugar (if needed)

100g ground almonds (preferably freshly ground)

1 level tablespoon tomato purée

3 tablespoons lemon juice

2 level teaspoons paprika

3 or 4 good pinches of cayenne pepper

4 tablespoons extra virgin olive oil

sea salt

Break apart the heads of garlic and give the cloves a bash so the peel comes off easily, but leave them whole. Peel the onion and chop roughly. Put the garlic cloves and onion into a large saucepan and add 300ml of the milk. Bring up to bubbling, then lower the heat, cover the pan and simmer very gently for about 25 minutes, until the garlic and onion are really soft.

Stir in the sugar and ground almonds, then tip the mixture into a food processor and whiz to a smooth paste. Return to the saucepan and stir in the remaining milk. Season generously with salt and bring to the boil, stirring. Now lower the heat and simmer very gently, stirring constantly, for 8–10 minutes. Pour into a bowl and leave until cold, then chill in the fridge.

Meanwhile, put the tomato purée, lemon juice, paprika and cayenne pepper into a small saucepan and heat until almost bubbling. Now stir over a low heat for about 3 minutes. Remove from the heat and leave until cold.

Spoon the chilled soup into individual bowls. Just before you eat, stir the olive oil vigorously into the cold tomato and paprika mixture and then spoon a whirl into the centre of each portion.

Perhaps the most unpleasant story of Bill's eating habits concerns surströmming, a fermented herring which he conceived a passion for during the war in Sweden. The fish are fermented in barrels for months and then tinned, where they continue fermenting until the tin bulges. Once opened, the pungent smell – a cross between open sewers and rotten egg – is almost unbearable, and to most people the taste is equally disgusting. But as with the Asian fruit durian, with its repulsive smell, some people become addicted to surströmming. Bill was one of them. When he left Sweden he brought a tin back and took it to a friend's flat where he was staying. The next morning, after a convivial evening, Bill woke to shouts of horror from his friend and a smell he knew well, but it was more overpowering than ever. The tin of surströmming had exploded in the heat of the sitting room, where

Bill had left it. Skeletons of the fish hung from the ceiling and the liquid had splashed all over the curtains and carpet. Cleaning proved impossible and Bill had to pay to replace the furnishings. A decade later Bill bought another tin of surstromming on a Swedish island where we went for a family holiday. From a distance, we watched him open it well away from the house where we were staying, but soon a dense black cloud of flies obliterated him.

We were always alone on the Lanzarote beaches, even if we stayed all day, but one summer in the mid 1960s a few young hippies set up camp at the far end of our favourite beach, Papagayo. As we sat eating our picnic or reading they walked amiably by, always naked, as Bill, to my constant embarrassment, was too. On the last day of the holiday, when we had packed up our picnic things, we climbed up onto the

Playa Blanca squid with sweet onions

My children always wanted Maria to cook them fried squid and chips, but in the earlier years she often prepared squid in another delicious way, which I have tried to reproduce here.

Serves 4–5

500g Spanish onions

2 level teaspoons coriander seeds

2 tablespoons olive oil

juice of 1 large orange

150ml unsweetened apple juice

2 rounded tablespoons tomato purée

1kg squid, cleaned (with tentacles)

2 rounded teaspoons dried oregano

sea salt, cayenne pepper

Peel and quarter the onions, then chop fairly small. Crush the coriander seeds finely, using a pestle and mortar. Heat the olive oil in a flameproof dish or wide pan over a medium heat. Add the onions and crushed coriander seeds and stir together for a minute or two. Now add the orange juice, apple juice and tomato purée.

Cover the dish and simmer very gently over the lowest possible heat for 30–40 minutes, stirring now and then until you have a soft, mushy sauce. Meanwhile, slice the squid bodies across in thin rings, but leave the tentacles whole.

Just before eating, season the sauce with salt and a few pinches of cayenne pepper and bring to the boil. Add the squid with the oregano, turn the heat down as low as possible and put the lid on. Cook for 2–4 minutes – only until the squid is just opaque. Take off the heat and serve at once.

headland where Bill had parked his battered Deux Chevaux. He had bought the car secondhand to keep on the island and it had parts literally tied together with string. As he was about to start the car, Bill hesitated and said he ought to say goodbye to the hippies. He was gone a long time. Worried that he might have had one of his accidents, we looked over the headland and saw him below talking intently to a very pretty naked girl. When he finally drove us home across the desert my mother chose to sit in the back and sniffed loudly all the way. 'Anything the matter Konko (his pet name for her)?' asked Bill.

Bill and my mother went to Playa Blanca for long periods until their old age, and Maria the cook stayed to the end. Lanzarote became a package-tour destination and even remote Playa Blanca had hotels and holiday complexes. Today it is built up all along the coast and Bill's house has become a boutique hotel, appropriately called 'La Casa del Embajador' (the house of the ambassador). In the mid 1970s when my husband David and I took our three young children to Lanzarote for the first time, Playa Blanca was still virtually untouched by tourism. We

Maria's fish albóndigas

Maria called these albóndigas, which usually means a type of meatball, but in fact they are more like fried fish quenelles. She used cooked fish left over from another meal and I would ask for them again and again. You need to start the preparation well ahead as it is done in stages, but it's well worth the effort and you can do most of it the day before if that is more convenient.

Serves 6

300–350g cooked boneless fish

2 medium onions

about 75g butter

2 heaped tablespoons plain flour, plus extra for coating

about 570ml whole milk

generous pinch of saffron strands

¼ nutmeg, grated

2 medium free-range eggs

sunflower or groundnut oil for shallow-frying

sea salt, black pepper

For the tomato sauce:

400g tin chopped tomatoes

1 level teaspoon harissa or chilli powder

1–2 tablespoons white wine vinegar

Remove any skin from the fish and flake the flesh small. Peel the onions and grate coarsely. Melt about two-thirds of the butter in a large, deep frying pan over a gentle heat. Add the grated onions and cook until they are transparent and pale golden. Add the remaining butter and once it has melted, add the flaked fish and stir to coat with butter. Remove from the heat and stir in the 2 heaped tablespoons flour with a wooden spoon.

Pour the milk into a saucepan, add the saffron and grated nutmeg, and season with salt and plenty of black pepper. Heat until bubbling and then gradually pour onto the fish and onion mixture, stirring all the time. Put the pan back over a medium heat and bring to a simmer, continuing to stir until the mixture is as thick as a soft dough. If it's too stiff, add a little more milk; if it isn't thick enough, mix a heaped teaspoon or so of flour with a little milk, add to the mixture and simmer again until thicker. Turn the mixture into a bowl and leave to cool, then cover and put in the fridge for at least 2 hours.

Shortly before you will be ready to eat, prepare the tomato sauce. Mash the chopped tomatoes thoroughly in a bowl with the harissa and wine vinegar, using a fork. Turn into a serving bowl.

Beat the eggs in a bowl. Using floured hands, take handfuls of the chilled fish mixture and form into small rissole shapes. Roll these on a well-floured board to coat in flour.

Heat a 1cm depth of oil in a clean, large, deep frying pan until it is almost smoking. You will need to fry the albóndigas in batches. Dip each one in the beaten egg and carefully lower into the oil. Fry them quickly until golden brown all over, then lift out with a slotted spoon or spatula and place on a double layer of kitchen paper to drain off excess oil. Once drained, transfer to a warmed serving dish.

Serve the albóndigas at once if possible, though they can be kept warm in a very low oven for half an hour or so. Put the tomato sauce on the table for people to spoon onto their albóndigas.

Canary cake

Maria made this gooey almond cake as a pudding, which she topped with bananas and a tangy orange syrup. You'll probably prefer crème fraîche to the tinned evaporated milk we poured onto it.

Serves 6–8

125g unskinned almonds

4 large free-range eggs, separated

75g golden caster sugar

finely grated rind of 2 large oranges

2 tablespoons warm water

pinch of salt

butter for greasing

For the syrup and topping:

juice of 2 large oranges

juice of ½ lemon

75g demerara sugar

1 level teaspoon ground cinnamon

3 small firm bananas

Heat the oven to 180°C/Gas 4. Butter a 20cm round cake tin and line the bottom with a disc of buttered baking parchment. Put the almonds in a food processor and grind finely.

In a large bowl, whisk the egg yolks with the caster sugar and orange rind until pale. Then gradually whisk in the ground almonds, followed by the warm water. In a clean bowl, whisk the egg whites with the salt until they stand in soft peaks. Using a metal spoon, gently fold them into the yolk mixture. Turn the mixture into the prepared tin and bake in the centre of the oven for 45–55 minutes until resistant to a very light touch in the centre.

While the cake is in the oven, make the syrup. Strain the orange and lemon juices through a sieve into a saucepan and add the demerara sugar and cinnamon. Stir over a low heat to dissolve the sugar, then increase the heat and boil briskly for 5 minutes. Remove from the heat and leave to cool.

When the cake is cooked, remove from the oven but leave it in the tin for 10 minutes; don't worry if it sinks slightly. Loosen the sides with a knife and turn out onto a serving plate. Peel the bananas, slice thinly and arrange in a jumble on top of the cake. Spoon the syrup over the bananas, allowing it to trickle down the sides of the cake. It is now ready to eat.

frequently came back from the beach for lunch. Swimming, sun and wind fired our appetites and Maria always prepared something good, but the children's firm favourite was squid and chips. Before supper in the evening we often watched Maria below the house leaping from rock to rock, swiftly knocking off limpets with a stone and collecting them in a bag. Back at the house she would mix chopped garlic and parsley with butter, put a blob on the flesh of each limpet and grill them briefly for our first course. It was Maria's equivalent to a plate of snails in France and, inexplicably, Lanzarote limpets were not tough.

Goats wandered about all over the desert and hills behind the village. I never discovered what they found to nibble on, but their owners clearly fed them well as they produced excellent cheese. The hill directly behind the village was so steep that it was more like a mountain and near the top, in a tiny house surrounded by goats, lived

a bent old lady who we bought cheeses from. I liked them best when they were squeaky fresh, still wet and white, with a tangy, salty taste. The size of a high cake and round, the cheeses were speckled with little holes. As they aged and became hard Maria used them in any dish that needed grated cheese. One evening, as we came down the mountain after a visit to the cheese lady, we heard singing coming from Salvador's café. As we walked in, we saw Salvador himself singing Spanish songs in a fine baritone voice, his wife Dolores joining in now and then. The rhythmic sound of the waves meeting the beach created a kind of accompaniment for the songs and the moon shone on the sea in a long streak. We sat in the café under the palm branch roof for some time, drinking the latest arrival of rough wine and tasting our new cheese. 'I love this place', said my mother, and for the rest of her life she seemed happier when she was in Lanzarote than anywhere else.

FIRST DISHES FROM A BASEMENT FLAT

As far back as my memory takes me, which is to my first school in Belgium when I was four years old, I have loved singing and in an early report the teacher wrote, *'Josceline a une très jolie voix.'* From the first time I sang a solo, aged nine, in the Christmas carol concert at boarding school, singing became known as 'my thing'. In rehearsals for school plays the producer would always say, 'Everyone must raise their voices – except Jossy.' I loved writing too, which is why I have a lifetime of densely scribbled diaries today, but I found cookery classes dismally dull and I rebelled against the teacher, Miss Gregson, known as Dregs, who put me at the bottom of the class.

In the early 1960s I was studying singing at the Guildhall School of Music in London. From one chaotic flat shared with five girls I moved into another with just one girlfriend, which felt very grown-up, even though we were only eighteen. The basement flat on Kensington Church Street was subterranean; if you looked up out of the front window you could just see the pavement above. We each paid £4 per week rent for a bedroom each, a musty windowless sitting room, and a kitchen like a small cupboard that we could hardly fit into at the same time. The kitchen was under the pavement so no fresh air or daylight came in and there wasn't an extractor to take away cooking

My first shepherd's pie

I've made countless variations of shepherd's pie but they all began with this, the first dish I ever made in the kitchen of my basement flat. Serve with a green vegetable or a simple green salad.

Serves 6–8

1kg potatoes

2 large onions

2 tablespoons vegetable oil

50g butter, cut roughly into cubes

800g–1kg minced lamb or beef

1 rounded teaspoon cumin seeds

2 teaspoons ground cinnamon

400g tin chopped tomatoes

2 medium free-range eggs

75g mature Cheddar or similar cheese, grated

a little milk

a little freshly grated Parmesan cheese

sea salt, black pepper

Peel the potatoes and steam or boil until cooked. Meanwhile, peel the onions and chop up fairly small. Heat 1 tablespoon oil in a large, deep frying pan and fry the onions over a fairly low heat until soft and slightly browned. Then, using a slotted spoon, transfer the onions to a plate and set aside. When the potatoes are cooked, drain and put them into a large bowl with the cubed butter; keep on one side.

Add the remaining oil to the empty frying pan and set over a fairly high heat. Add the minced meat with the cumin seeds, ground cinnamon, a generous sprinkling of salt and plenty of black pepper. As the meat browns, dig at it with a wooden spoon to separate it.

When the minced meat is well separated and browned, add the fried onions and the chopped tomatoes and mix well. Transfer to a large, fairly shallow ovenproof dish and spread level. Heat the oven to 180°C/Gas 4.

Now mash the potatoes. Beat the eggs in a bowl using a fork and add them to the mashed potatoes with the grated Cheddar and a good sprinkling of pepper. Mix together thoroughly and then add a little milk to make the mash a little less firm than usual. Spoon evenly over the meat and sprinkle with a little grated Parmesan. Cook in the centre of the oven for 40 minutes to 1 hour until the mash topping is golden brown.

smells and grease; the walls dripped with damp, there was a dented, chipped and rusty enamel gas cooker, and a cracked china sink with shelves above. Despite this we wanted to entertain and cook meals for friends. Our first attempt, when we cooked spaghetti for nine people who crammed into the tiny sitting room, was secretly a disaster. As we drained the spaghetti into a colander it overflowed into the grubby sink and started slithering down the plughole. We pulled as much of it back as we could, piled it into a bowl with some tinned tomato sauce and, admitting nothing, proudly took it through to our hungry friends.

I was longing to cook properly, hoping I would be able to recapture tastes I had discovered during my childhood abroad. I didn't have a cookery book so it was trial and error; something I have always felt helped me in a way, because I had to rely on my memories and imagination, rather than be reined in by recipe rules. As I lived on an allowance of £10 a week for my rent, food, clothes and anything else, ingredients had to be cheap. The first thing I cooked was a Shepherd's pie. I was determined it shouldn't be like the grey, watery mince we had at school, so to recreate the flavour of Syrian minced lamb dishes I'd enjoyed, I added some cumin seeds and cinnamon I found in a delicatessen down the road, and copied Granny by adding cheese to the mashed potato. It was a success, and from then on I was keen to experiment more. I discovered I could buy wood pigeons for a shilling each, so I casseroled them slowly with onions and carrots, throwing in a tin of petits pois at the last moment; it seemed a luxury to have a whole bird each. A real coup was finding cod's cheeks in the fishmonger at sixpence a pound; they were fine textured with a delicate flavour and, once fried, tasted like expensive scampi.

My singing teacher at the Guildhall, Emilie Hooke, was ageing and large, with salt-and-pepper hair piled up in a bun, a big pale face, small kind eyes and eyebrows drawn in a pencil-thin black line. In her youth she had been a pupil of Sir Henry Wood, the famous conductor associated with the Promenade concerts at the Albert Hall, who had left her his piano. I always wondered why he did this, as she played clumsily, but she was a warm, encouraging woman and chose interesting things for me to sing. I loved the poignant songs of Henri Duparc, the brilliant nineteenth-century composer. Miss Hooke liked hearing about the ups and downs of my life. I was in the throes of my first love affair with a clever, willowy undergraduate who said he had an incurable brain disease, though it seemed to be the excuse for times he was not particularly attentive to me. When Miss Hooke could see I was upset she would make me pour my heart into Chanson Triste, Extase or Lamento by Duparc, and I would feel much better. One evening I came back to the basement flat and found my girlfriend full of alarm, having discovered that a man had climbed through my bedroom window and was lying 'dead', she said, on my bed. It turned out to be my boyfriend, dead drunk, but his excuse later was his brain disease.

To give me a feeling of home and security I filled my bedroom with little pictures and pretty Victorian objects, which you could buy for a few shillings in junk shops. I planted herbs in a window box on my windowsill for cooking – at that time the only herbs sold in shops were dried and often the only option was a drum of dried mixed herbs. My room was at the back of the building and looked onto a dark passage full of dustbins that we had to walk down from the street to get to the door of our flat. From my window I could see railings above and a strip of green that was part of the communal gardens behind. For only half-an-hour a day during the summer, if it was fine, a shaft of sunlight hit my window box. Nevertheless, my herbs survived and I was able to throw fresh mint into dishes to lend some Middle-Eastern character.

My love affair with the willowy boyfriend (pictured with me on page 68) dragged on unsatisfactorily for more than two years. I pined when on holiday in Lanzarote, wrote reams about my emotional agony and uncertainty in my diary, and waited for the telephone to ring in London. I cried as often as my mother. At the Guildhall I sang my Duparc songs

with even more passion, as well as Italian arias about the pain of love and loss. I had quite a busy life with my friends, and several other men (boys as I still called them then) showed interest, but I was convinced that I would never be able to love anyone who wasn't six-foot-four and gauntly thin with long legs, long sensitive fingers, a long face with deep-set, searching eyes and full lips, who knew all about the Spanish Civil War, recited Lorca poetry and listened to Thelonius Monk. I bought a black kitten for luck and company in my room at night.

Months later I came back to the flat with a new boyfriend after having dinner at The Ark, a popular restaurant up the road near Notting Hill Gate, which is still there today. If someone invited me

Oxtail with cider, prunes and beans

I was thrilled to discover that such a cheap cut of meat produced a dish so rich in flavour, and delighted to find that it tasted even better if made conveniently ahead and reheated the following day. Serve with mashed potato, which is lovely with the juices, and a green salad.

Serves 6

3 large onions

2 tablespoons sunflower or groundnut oil

about 1kg oxtail pieces

100g pitted prunes

450ml dry cider

coarsely grated rind and juice of 1 large orange

1 rounded teaspoon juniper berries

3–4 large cloves garlic

400g tin chopped tomatoes

400g tin haricot beans, drained

about 10 sage leaves

sea salt, black pepper

Heat the oven to 240°C/Gas 9. Peel and halve the onions, then slice across. Heat the oil in a large frying pan over a medium-high heat and fry the oxtail pieces, in batches, until well browned all over. Using a slotted spatula, transfer the oxtail to a large casserole dish. Now add the onions to the frying pan and fry until soft and browned, then add to the casserole.

Cut the prunes in half and add them to the casserole with the cider, grated orange rind and juice, and the juniper berries. Season with salt and plenty of coarsely ground black pepper. Put the lid on.

Cook the casserole on the centre shelf of the oven for about 20 minutes until the liquid is bubbling. Then lower the oven setting to 140°C/Gas 1 and cook for a further 2½ hours or until the meat is very soft and starting to come away from the bones.

Now peel the garlic, slice the cloves thinly crossways and add to the casserole with the chopped tomatoes, haricot beans and whole sage leaves. Return to the oven for another 45 minutes. Leave until cold and then refrigerate or keep in a cold larder until the next day.

The next day, spoon off the solidified fat from the top of the stew, put the lid back on and reheat the stew in a hot oven at 240°C/Gas 9 for 20–30 minutes until bubbling. Adjust the seasoning before serving if necessary.

Simple fish stew with bay leaves

I bought my fish in Mac Fisheries at the top of Kensington Church Street. At that time cod was cheap, but the only peppers available were green ones and olive oil was tricky to find except in chemists, so I used butter instead. Now I always use olive oil and red peppers. Serve with potatoes to mop up the juices, and a green vegetable.

Serves 4–5

500g–750g cod, haddock or hake fillet, skinned

3–4 bay leaves (fresh or dried)

4–5 tomatoes (plum variety if available)

1 pointed red pepper

4 tablespoons extra virgin olive oil

juice of 1 lemon

1 tablespoon fresh orange juice

sea salt, black pepper

Heat the oven to 150°C/Gas 2. Cut the fish into large chunks. Using a small sharp knife, make an incision in each piece of fish and insert a broken piece of bay leaf. Arrange the fish in a wide, fairly shallow casserole dish and sprinkle with salt and plenty of black pepper.

Slice the tomatoes across thinly. Cut the pepper in half lengthways, discard the seeds and stem, and slice across as finely as you possibly can.

Arrange the sliced tomatoes and pepper over the fish. Pour the olive oil, lemon juice and orange juice over the top, cover the dish and cook in the centre of the oven for 50–60 minutes until the fish is just cooked through.

Almond and lemon cake

This was the first cake I ever made. The recipe, given to me by the German mother of a school friend, was surprisingly moist and light, even cooked in our wonky oven. I could only find ground almonds then, but grinding unskinned almonds adds texture. It's a good cake to serve with a fruity dessert. Have the butter at room temperature.

Serves 6

75g unskinned almonds

110g unsalted butter, plus extra for greasing

150g golden caster sugar

3 medium free-range eggs

40g self-raising flour, plus extra for dusting

finely grated rind and juice of 1 small lemon

icing sugar for dusting

Heat the oven to 180°C/Gas 4. Butter the sides of an 18cm sandwich tin and dust with flour. Line the bottom of the tin with a disc of baking parchment. Grind the almonds in a food processor as finely as you can.

Whisk the butter and sugar together in a bowl until light and fluffy. Whisk in the eggs and ground almonds alternately, whisking well between each addition. Then fold in the flour with a metal spoon, followed by the lemon rind. Lastly, gradually fold in the lemon juice. Turn the mixture into the prepared tin and bake in the centre of the oven for 45–50 minutes.

Leave the cake to cool in the tin, then loosen the sides with a knife and turn the cake out onto a serving plate. Sift a little icing sugar over the surface.

out to dinner I usually suggested The Ark. It was friendly and romantic with candles on the red-and-white-check tablecloths, and I loved their French onion soup, which cost two shillings and sixpence. You took your own wine. The lady chef, a Hungarian called Mrs Vig, made a good goulash, which glowed like a flame with paprika, and I always chose either chocolate mousse or a frothy lemon syllabub for pudding. That night, the new boyfriend, a charming womaniser, paid me lots of compliments and the large sum of nearly £3 for our three-course dinner because he had ordered the most expensive dish, steak au poivre.

It had been raining heavily while we were eating and, full of red wine, we almost slipped at the steep end of Kensington Church Street. As we turned down the steps to the passageway that led to my flat, we realised that there must have been a torrential downpour, causing a flood, as water was pouring down the hill and overflowing into the basement areas of the houses. We waded along the passage, squeezing past the dustbins, and opened the door of the flat. The corridor and all the rooms were under about two feet of water. A few potato peelings from the kitchen floor floated towards us. In my bedroom, on top of the wardrobe, sat my little black cat, ears back, eyes open wide as she looked down at the lake beneath her, opening and closing her mouth in a silent mew for help, having totally lost her voice with fear.

Dried apricot tart

The basement flat was the start of my love affair with upside-down tarts, which are so easy, and the pastry beneath never soggy as it has been cooked on top. For appearance, I like to use the orange-coloured dried apricots here, rather than the natural dark brown ones. Serve the tart with crème fraîche.

Serves 8

For the short pastry:

200g plain flour

160g cold unsalted butter, cubed

pinch of salt

5–6 tablespoons ice-cold water

For the filling:

250g ready-to-eat dried apricots

50g unsalted butter (at room temperature)

100g golden caster sugar

finely grated rind of 1 orange

melted butter for brushing

To make the pastry, tip the flour and butter into a food processor and pulse a few times until the butter is roughly incorporated into the flour and the mixture resembles coarse breadcrumbs; don't over-process – there should still be small pieces of butter visible. Add enough water to just bring the pastry together, pulsing very briefly. Tip the pastry out onto a work surface and bring together into a ball. Wrap in cling film and rest in the fridge for about an hour before using.

In the meantime, soak the dried apricots in warm water to cover for about 30 minutes. Heat the oven to 200°C/Gas 6.

Smear the bottom and sides of a 25cm round flan dish (not a loose-based one) with the butter. Sprinkle the caster sugar all over the butter and scatter the grated orange rind on top. Drain the apricots; they will probably be whole, so open them up to make two halves. Arrange the apricots outer side down in neat circles on top of the butter and sugar mixture.

Roll the pastry out on a lightly floured surface to a round, a little larger than the size of the flan dish. Lift the pastry over the filled flan dish and press the overlapping edges firmly down inside the edge of the dish. Brush the pastry with a little melted butter and pierce with a knife or skewer, making two or three holes to let steam escape.

Bake the tart in the centre of the oven for 25 minutes, then lower the setting to 150°C/Gas 2 and bake for a further 35–40 minutes. Leave the tart to cool slightly, then turn out upside-down onto a flat serving plate. Eat while still warm.

LAST JOURNEY OF THE ORIENT EXPRESS

In March 1964 my friend Elizabeth's rich father offered to finance a month's holiday for both of us in Turkey, including first-class tickets on the legendary Orient Express from Paris to Istanbul. As a twenty-year-old student living on £10 a week, I could not believe my luck. We travelled to Paris on the boat train from Victoria station, and reached the Gare-de-l'Est in time for the evening departure of the famous train, with its distinctive dark blue and gold carriages. Anticipating glamour and romance, we searched for our first-class cabin. As expected, it had French-polished mahogany walls and brass fitments, a banquette sofa which turned into two comfortable bunks at night, and a table with a decorative lamp, but it all looked a bit faded, and worse, there was nowhere to wash except a small cold water basin in the lavatory at the far end of the carriage.

But it was nearly three days of haute cuisine and drinking fine wine from crystal glasses that we were most looking forward to. We had imagined ourselves in the ornate dining car, lit by little silk-shaded table lamps, with silver tableware, huge linen napkins and bone china crockery, meeting some fascinating and distinguished

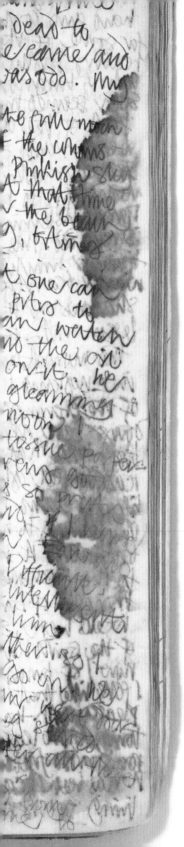

fellow passengers. However, our expectations were shattered when the conductor informed us as the train was about to leave that from this week the dining carriage had been withdrawn, and there was no drinking water. From now on passengers would have to bring their own food and drink. All we had was a packet of Ryvita and two boxes of processed cheese triangles. The conductor pointed through the window to a stall on the platform and said we had just enough time to buy some bottles of mineral water. So, instead of the glittering journey we had anticipated on the original Paris-Istanbul route of the Orient Express, we were to experience the start of its death.

It was grey and rainy as we rattled through Italy the next day, then the mysterious countries of Communist Yugoslavia and Bulgaria, and I noted in my diary that we were 'bored, dirty and hungry'. As I took out the large leather-bound book that evening to write again I found that one of the bottles of mineral water stored in my case had exploded and soaked four years of emotional outpourings, almost obliterating much of the writing with water marks. This, I wrote when the pages had dried, was 'the worst thing that could happen', and I was only slightly cheered when some friendly Turkish passengers gave us halva crammed with pistachios. Otherwise our 'horrible little meals' were composed of anything we could buy at the few stations where we stopped briefly en route, and there was nothing warm to comfort us.

On the morning of the third day we woke to hot sunshine at last. We had crossed the Turkish frontier during the night and were looking out at an endless plain. There were little children playing by the railway line, low wooden houses and some horses and carts. Women wearing baggy Turkish trousers and shepherd boys dressed in skins (pictured right) were working in the fields, a scene that looked like a nineteenth-century painting. We arrived at Istanbul in the afternoon where we were booked into the legendary Pera Palas Hotel that overlooks the Golden Horn. We walked into the marble hall to find the place empty; there were no statesmen, no famous musicians or writers, no billionaires or stars of stage and screen, and no spies. The ornate decorations, furnishings and Turkish rugs looked unchanged since the 1890s, simply faded and dusty. We appeared to be the only people apart from the hotel staff. Ceremoniously the uniformed lift-boy opened the gate of an outsized lift of polished brass, iron filigree and glass; it was like a gilded cage for giant birds.

Our room on the sixth floor was light and spacious, with two large brass bedsteads and a huge marble bathroom, where we immediately washed off three days of grime. Still feeling somewhat bewildered, we set off for a walk. The backlit skyline of domes and minarets seen over the water, and the crooked cobbled streets with fragile-looking old wooden houses on each side, gave us even more a feeling of the exotic East. Almost at once we were surrounded by men, who walked alongside and followed us persistently. Naive as we were, we had not realised that in a Muslim country unused to tourism, the sight of two young girls in mini-skirts, walking alone through the streets, would be bound to cause a stir. On our way back to the hotel, a man pinched Elizabeth's bottom, another hit him and a fight started. We quickly walked away. 'I feel our time in Turkey will be more of an adventure than we had anticipated,' I wrote apprehensively in my diary.

That night, not daring to go out again, we sat at a table in the centre of the palatial dining hall of the hotel under a grandiose chandelier. Far from us, a line of waiters in black-tail suits, tightly knotted black bow ties and starched white shirts looked at us curiously. We were the only diners, and the silence was unnerving. One of the waiters, who looked very old, slowly shuffled towards us across the great expanse of floor with a menu. Our spirits soared; it would be our first real meal for nearly four days. It took the bent old waiter a long time to bring us our starter of *yalanci dolma* (stuffed vine leaves) on a large tray, but they were worth waiting for – the leaves unusually tender and filled with perfectly cooked rice, sweet onions, tiny currants, plenty of pine kernels and fresh dill. For my main course, I chose what seemed to be a rather better, lighter version of a Greek moussaka, which I decided I must try and reproduce when I got back to England. At the end of the meal, the crisp, honey-soaked, walnut-laden baklava was also far superior to any we had eaten in London's Greek student restaurants. The old waiter said of course this was so, as baklava and most other dishes found in Greece originated in Turkey. I didn't need persuading, I had decided that Turkish food was going to be one of the best things about our journey.

We did not know it but a contact given to me by a friend in London was going to transform our Turkish adventure. Emin Dirvana arrived at the hotel in a tweed jacket, holding a pale brown gabardine

Pera Palas pie

This recipe, a sort of Turkish shepherd's pie, is drawn from memory of the first meal I had in Turkey, in the empty dining room of the historic hotel. Once made, it can be kept and reheated at any time over the next few days.

Serves 6

1 large aubergine, about 350g

lemon juice or white wine vinegar for sprinkling

3 tablespoons olive oil

30g pine kernels

2 large cloves garlic

500g lean minced lamb

2 teaspoons paprika

good handful of dill

50g plain flour

600ml whole milk

250g curd or other soft white cheese

sea salt, black pepper

Cut the aubergine across into roughly 1cm thick slices and smear all over with lemon juice or vinegar. Sprinkle with salt and leave to drain in a colander in the sink for half an hour.

Rinse the aubergine slices under cold running water to remove the salt, pat well dry with kitchen paper and cut into small cubes. Heat 2 tablespoons of the olive oil in a large frying pan over a high heat, add the aubergines and stir around for a few minutes until soft and browned. Tip onto a plate.

Set aside 1 level tablespoonful of the pine kernels. Tip the rest into the frying pan, stir for a minute or two until browned and then tip them onto the plate with the fried aubergines. Peel and finely chop the garlic.

Add the remaining 1 tablespoon olive oil to the frying pan over a high heat. Add the minced lamb and stir it around, breaking it up, until browned and any liquid has evaporated. Add the chopped garlic and paprika, stir for a minute or two and then remove the pan from the heat. Lastly, chop the dill and stir into the meat with a sprinkling of sea salt and black pepper. Turn into a wide, fairly shallow ovenproof dish. Heat the oven to 190°C/Gas 5.

To make the topping, tip the flour into a cold saucepan and stir in 2–3 tablespoons of the milk with a wooden spoon to make a smooth paste. Stir in the remaining milk, put the pan over the heat and bring to the boil, stirring all the time. Let it bubble, still stirring, for 2–3 minutes. Remove from the heat, add the curd cheese and stir or whisk until thoroughly blended into the sauce. Season to taste with salt and black pepper.

Now stir in the reserved fried aubergines and pine kernels and pour the topping over the lamb in the dish. Scatter the reserved pine kernels on top. Bake the pie towards the top of the oven for about 30 minutes until the topping is browned.

mackintosh and a copy of The Times, and took us out to dinner. He was a tall man with wavy grey hair and a neat moustache, a big face, smiling eyes, a wide smile, and the largest nose I've ever seen. Emin's manners were impeccable and his English was almost too perfect. An ex-soldier and diplomat, and a confirmed bachelor who had ancestors in the Ottoman court, he knew everything about Turkey, and its history and architecture. Aware that Elizabeth was half-Russian, he took us to the atmospheric Russian restaurant, Rejans, founded by Russian exiles in 1932, and still run at that time by two ancient Russian women who had been there since after the revolution. Like the Pera Palas, diplomats, statesmen, spies and writers had frequented the restaurant over the years, but that night they seemed mostly to be ageing white Russians. One old woman, sitting alone at the next table, sang snatches of Russian songs between mouthfuls of blini.

Emin Bey, as he was addressed, lived in Kabrisli Yalisi, the largest of the eighteenth-century wooden summerhouses, called *yalis*, to survive on the Bosphorus. Situated on the Asian bank but built out over the water, it was bought, enlarged and transformed in 1840 by Emin's great-grandfather Kibrizli-Mehmed-Emin-Pasha, who was Grand

Below: Emin Dirvana in his summer garden at Kibrisli Yalisi. Right: The winter garden room of Kibrisli Yalisi.

Meatballs with egg and lemon sauce

This is Emin's recipe. It's a peasant dish, which he first tasted as a child when he went into the kitchen and found the servants of the house eating it. He always preferred it to the chef's grander creations.

Serves 4

good handful of flat-leafed parsley

1 medium onion

500g lean minced lamb

100g long-grain rice

1 litre chicken stock

1 large free-range egg

juice of 2 lemons

100ml water

4 level teaspoons plain flour

25g butter

1 rounded teaspoon paprika

sea salt, black pepper

Pull the leaves off the parsley stems and chop them finely. Peel the onion and chop finely. Put the mince in a bowl and mix in the chopped parsley and onion, the rice and a good seasoning of salt and black pepper. Using wet hands, form the mixture into little balls, about the size of a small marble.

Bring the stock to the boil in a large saucepan, then drop in the meatballs. As it returns to the boil, remove any scum from the surface with a metal spoon. Lower the heat, cover and simmer very gently for 30 minutes.

In a small saucepan, whisk the egg with the lemon juice and water. Sift in the flour and whisk until smooth. Place over a medium heat and slowly bring to the boil, stirring with a wooden spoon; if the sauce gets too thick to stir easily, add a little more water. Now gradually stir the sauce into the meatball pan and spoon carefully into a round, heated serving dish.

Before serving, melt the butter with the paprika in a small saucepan over a low heat. Stir around for 3 minutes, then trickle over the meatballs.

Vizier to the Sultan Abdulmecid and to his successor Abdulaziz. Emin told us a story about how he had inherited his nose. He explained that his grandmother had been a pretty fourteen-year-old girl in the harem at Topkapi Palace when Sultan Abdulhamid 1 noticed her and asked her to sit on his lap. But when asked to kiss him she refused, telling him she didn't like him because his nose was too big. 'In that case,' replied the Sultan, who had sixteen wives, 'you will be married to the person in my court with the largest nose.' This happened to be Emin's grandfather, who was a young military attaché at the time, and to everyone's surprise the marriage proved to be a true love match.

Emin shared the house with his three brothers, two sisters and their families; fifteen of them altogether, but it would have been more in the past. There was a vast grand main hall once used as a ballroom, as well as other reception rooms, three kitchens and two dining rooms, dating back to the days when female members of the family never ate with guests. The harem, or women's quarters, were in a wing on one side, and still used as such by Emin's grandmother until her death in

the 1920s. It was a cool day, so Emin suggested we ate lunch in the winter garden – a large and spectacular glass room with an intricate mosaic floor of black and white marble pebbles and a fountain in the centre. Here, and on a subsequent visit at a table in the waterfront garden, we realised that Emin was a true gastronome. We were treated to smoked sturgeon and eel, *lakerda* (raw fish preserved in olive oil and lemon juice), large and tender mussels fried briefly in featherlight beer batter, a succulent mussel stew, grated courgette fritters, Emin's own little meatballs in an egg and lemon sauce, a syrup-infused semolina and almond cake made by Emin's sister-in-law, and little triangles of crispy yufka pastry filled with white cheese and parsley – the best *borek* I have eaten to this day.

We ventured alone to the food markets of Istanbul and marvelled at the mountains of glossy, plump dried fruit and enormous walnuts. Particularly spectacular were silver swordfish, arranged in large circles on sticks, like Catherine wheels on November 5th, and so sparkling fresh that they really did look like fireworks. We nibbled *simit*, the traditional round breads covered with sesame seeds, which were piled high on carts and on a tray on the seller's head. And we sipped *salep*, a glutinous hot drink made from a root and flavoured strongly with cinnamon, which was carried through the market in an urn strapped to the seller's back. But it was at Konyali's, the businessmen's restaurant near the station, with Emin, where I first tried *tavuk gogsu kazandibi*, a pudding made with chicken breast, of all unlikely things. It looked like many Turkish milk puddings with a caramelised top – you would never guess that it had anything to do with chicken – but the texture was so special. The chicken used, which has to be just killed and still warm, adds a sensation of silk fine threads to the creaminess that is unique and irresistible. I became almost addicted to it.

Everyone told us we had to go to Pandeli's, a restaurant still well known today above Istanbul's spice market near the Galata bridge. By now we knew that the aubergine is to Turkey what the leek is to Wales and we were bowled over by their *patlican salata* – the famous smoky flavoured aubergine purée made with sunflower instead of olive oil to keep it light – and a hot version to which they added butter and cheese. We also loved the tarama, a far cry from more familiar, commercially produced, pink taramasalata with its pasty texture. The Pandeli version, made from the salted roe of the grey mullet rather than smoked cod's roe was almost white, with a grainy consistency. To Emin's delight, we ate everything we were offered; huge orange mussels from the Bosphorus stuffed with pine kernels, *levrek kagitta* (sea bass cooked in paper), lamb and aubergine kebabs and a velvety spinach purée. And we still had room for *ekmek kadayifi*, a famous Turkish pudding of

Kibrisli cake

This is my recreation of a cake made by Emin's sister-in-law at their joint family home on the Bosphorus, Kibrisli Yalisi. I like it best served as a pudding with a bowl of soft fruit and some whole milk yogurt or crème fraîche.

Serves 8–10

5 large free-range eggs, separated

250g golden caster sugar

finely grated rind of 1 lemon

125g semolina

125g ground almonds

pinch of baking powder

150ml water

¼ level teaspoon salt

1 level tablespoon sesame seeds

butter for greasing

For the syrup:

175g golden granulated or caster sugar

2 tablespoons honey

just under 300ml water

juice of 1 lemon

To finish:

1 level tablespoon sesame seeds

Heat the oven to 180°C/Gas 4. Lightly butter a deep 20cm round cake tin (not one with a loose base) and line with a disc of greaseproof paper. In a large bowl, whisk the egg yolks, caster sugar and grated lemon rind together until very pale. Then add the semolina, ground almonds, baking powder and water and whisk until smooth.

In a clean bowl, whisk the egg whites with the salt until they stand in soft peaks. Using a metal spoon, fold them gently into the yolk mixture and then pour into the prepared cake tin. Sprinkle the sesame seeds lightly over the surface and bake in the centre of the oven for 40–50 minutes or until the cake feels firm to a gentle touch in the middle.

While the cake is in the oven, make the syrup. Put the granulated sugar, honey and water into a saucepan. Stir over a low heat to dissolve, then increase the heat and boil briskly, without stirring, for 4–5 minutes. Remove from the heat, pour in the lemon juice through a sieve and stir in. Stand the pan in a sink of cold water to cool.

Once cooked, stand the cake in its tin on a wire rack. Spoon the cold syrup slowly and evenly over the hot cake, letting it soak in. Leave until cold, then carefully run a knife around the inside of the tin and turn the cake out; you may have to shake the tin to release it. Turn the cake the right way up onto a serving plate and sprinkle with the sesame seeds.

Bosphorus mussel stew

The mussels in the Bosphorus in front of Emin's house were large, plump and deep orange, yet sweet and tender. On a warm day in his garden we ate a cold stew of mussels something like this – Emin called it a salad. You can serve it hot or cold, but not chilled.

Serves 6

500–600g aubergines

lemon juice or wine vinegar for sprinkling

1kg fresh mussels

300ml water

250g small red onions

2 large cloves garlic

400g tin chopped tomatoes

2 rounded tablespoons tomato purée

3 tablespoons extra virgin olive oil

1 rounded tablespoon pine kernels

good handful of dill leaves

sea salt, black pepper

Cut the aubergines across into fairly thick slices and then halve the slices, sprinkling them with lemon juice or wine vinegar as you do so. Rub all over with salt and put into a colander in the sink.

Wash the mussels and scrub them if they are dirty. Pour the water into a large saucepan and bring to the boil over a high heat. Add the mussels, cover with a tight-fitting lid and cook for about 2 minutes until all the shells have opened. Pour the liquid from the mussels into a fairly large flameproof casserole. Extract the mussels from their shells and put them into a bowl, discarding any that haven't opened. Cover and set aside.

Rinse the aubergines under cold running water to remove the salt. Peel the onions and slice finely into rings. Peel the garlic and slice finely across.

Bring the mussel liquid up to the boil and add the aubergines, onions, garlic, chopped tomatoes, tomato purée, olive oil and a generous sprinkling of black pepper. Stir to mix, then cover the casserole and simmer as gently as possible on the hob for about 40 minutes, stirring now and then.

Taste and adjust the seasoning if necessary, adding salt only if needed. Add the mussels to the casserole and then take off the heat.

Put a small dry frying pan over the heat, toss in the pine kernels and toast for a minute to brown, then tip them into the dish.

Chop the dill and throw it into the mussel stew as you serve it, or if eating cold, stir the dill in when the dish has cooled and trickle a little more olive oil over the top.

light-textured bread infused with a sticky sugar syrup and filled with *kaymak*, the Turkish version of clotted cream made from the cream of buffalo milk. Finally we rolled out of the restaurant into the teeming, noisy scene of bewildering activity outside.

There were people, cars, bicycles, pigeons and food everywhere, and a row of busy restaurants under the Galata bridge, which joined the Asian and European sides of Istanbul. Hundreds of gleaming boats bobbed up and down on the Bosphorus, and hundreds of people crowded round them. In each boat was a mound of freshly caught fish and a charcoal brazier, with fishermen, boatmen and cooks all shouting, '*Balik ekmek! Balik ekmek!*' Within minutes, the absolutely fresh fish were fried quickly, put into half a loaf of bread and given to the waiting customers. In the restaurants we saw *uskumru dolmasi*; these looked like whole fried mackerel, but their flesh, skeleton and small bones had been skillfully removed through the head and the empty skin stuffed with the chopped mackerel flesh mixed with onions, walnuts, pine kernels, spices and herbs. This was a fascinating area of Istanbul that we could hardly bear to leave for our afternoon of sightseeing. By the time we had been round the Blue Mosque there was a purply pink sunset behind the minarets.

Emin was as knowledgeable a guide to the old mosques, Islamic buildings and classical ruins of Turkey as he was to the food. He suggested a two-day trip to Bursa, the first capital of the Ottoman Empire, reached from Istanbul by crossing the Sea of Marmara by boat. In the spring of 1964 Bursa was wonderfully peaceful; a beautiful old Turkish town on the green lower slopes of the still snow-capped Mount Uludag, with olive groves and orchards of fruit trees coming into pink and white blossom all around. There weren't any modern buildings in the town, just lovely wooden houses, alluring old mosques and muslim graves. In the cobbled streets, instead of cars were donkeys, horses and carts, many curious children and hundreds of cats. Round the fountains in the courtyards of the mosques sat rows of old men in caps (pictured left), eager to ask Emin about the two young foreign girls with him. It seemed a perfect escape from the crowds and noise of Istanbul. And there was culinary interest here too.

Bursa was the birthplace of the doner kebab, known as *Iskender kebab*, after the chef, Iskender Efendi, who, in 1867, invented the method of roasting lamb in front of upright charcoal on a large vertical spit. Quite unlike the dense, dry fast-food version sold in Britain, the *Iskender kebab* was made of large pieces of tender, juicy lamb, fragrant from the thyme-covered hills nearby. Packed on a hand-turned spit, the delectable lamb was sliced off in long slivers as the outside cooked, and served coated with yogurt and melted butter, along with a fresh

tomato sauce. I had never tasted anything quite like it, and since that visit to Bursa any other doner kebab has been a disappointment.

On our return to Istanbul we told Emin that we planned to travel by bus down to the south of Turkey via Izmir and the ruins of Ephesus, along the Mediterranean coast and up again through the centre across the plains. He was horrified. 'But it is too dangerous for women alone, and you don't speak Turkish.' He was right; almost the only tourists in the south of Turkey in the early 1960s were guided groups visiting the ancient ruins, and recently a girl had been murdered on a beach. In Emin's kind and gallant way he said, 'I will accompany you.' This was even kinder than he intended. He wanted to hire a car but we insisted on travelling by rickety local buses, and made him stay in crumbling caravanserais with minimal washing facilities 'for the atmosphere'.

But Emin put up with it all and we had an incredible three-week journey, wandering amongst the deserted ruins of Ephesus and Side, with poppies and wild flowers growing amongst them, eating fresh strawberries for tea in the heady scent of roses and orange blossom that hung over the lively port of Antalya, swimming in the sea beside the Crusader castle of Anamur, watching the Whirling Dervishes in dusty Konya, and more. Chaperoned by Emin we could enjoy evenings in restaurants and bars, full of inquisitive but friendly men, where we could not have gone alone. Here we listened to mournful songs and

Above, Beautiful Bursa, a peaceful old town steeped in history. Below, Head of Medusa, Ephesus.

Muhalebi with orange blossom syrup

I love the rose and orange blossom flavoured milky puddings of Turkey and the Middle East. I top my version of Muhalebi with an orange blossom flavoured syrup and chopped pistachios.

Serves 6

25g cornflour

700ml whole milk

50g caster sugar

2 tablespoons rose water

50g ground almonds

For the syrup:

4 tablespoons water

120g caster sugar

2 tablespoons orange flower water

1 tablespoon lemon juice, strained

15g shelled pistachio nuts (unsalted), to finish

In a cup, blend the cornflour with 1 tablespoon of the milk to a smooth paste. Pour the remaining milk into a saucepan and bring almost to the boil. Briskly stir in the cornflour paste and bring to the boil, stirring constantly.

Simmer, stirring, for 2–3 minutes, then add the sugar and rose water. Continue to simmer and stir for another minute, then stir in the ground almonds. Pour the mixture into six small serving bowls and set aside to cool.

To make the syrup, put the water and sugar into a saucepan and dissolve over a low heat, stirring. Bring to the boil and boil for 1–2 minutes, without stirring, then remove from the heat and stir in the orange flower water and lemon juice. Let cool slightly for 2–3 minutes.

Spoon the syrup over the cold puddings. Chop the pistachios roughly and sprinkle them on top. Chill the puddings in the fridge for at least an hour before serving.

music played on unfamiliar Turkish instruments, and the men would often get up spontaneously and dance. Late at night when we left they would crowd round to kiss our hands.

Before we left Istanbul, by air for the return journey, I went to the market and bought twelve jars of rose petal jam. The delicately scented taste and squeaking consistency of the petals suspended in the pink syrup reminded me of the Damask roses in Syria, and I still think rose petal jam stirred into yogurt beats honey any day. Luckily, in those pre-terrorist days, you could take anything as hand luggage so the jam reached England intact. Emin led us through the chaos of the airport, carrying my heavy bag of jam as far as he was allowed. He kissed our hands as we left, then placed them on his forehead, which he told us was a custom used for the old and revered, or for princesses. I turned back as we went through the gate and saw him looking sad. From then on he and I, both compulsive letter writers, corresponded regularly, until his death over three decades later, and whenever I returned to Turkey I visited him. He was a very special friend indeed.

ELECTRIC SHOCKS
ON THE
WEST SIDE

I had a one-day honeymoon. It was January 1967 and my boyfriend David, a young television reporter working in America at that time for CBS Television, was at the end of his Christmas holiday in England. It came as a happy surprise when he asked me if I would marry him before he returned to New York, particularly as I had always been apprehensive of the tensions the long run-up to a big wedding might bring. His proposal came in the early hours of Wednesday morning, we were married in a London registry office on Friday, held an informal party at his place that evening and then, after a perfect day and night in a country hotel, my new husband flew back over the ocean. Two weeks later, after packing up my flat and leaving my job on a magazine, I joined him in the Big Apple.

The initial experience of arriving in New York was as thrilling as it is today, and all the more different from England then: the extraordinary light and energy; the sculptural beauty of the early skyscrapers; the size of the smart East Side department stores and their wealth of merchandise; the orgy of lights in Times Square; Chinatown with its colourful restaurants, exotic shops and firework displays; Greenwich Village with artists, beat poets, folk musicians, cultural cafés and coffee

The views up and down the Hudson river from our apartment on the West Side.

houses; restaurants of every nationality with authentic food; and the musicals on Broadway that had no equal in England – neither the vibrancy of the show nor the enthusiasm of the audience.

Further up off Broadway, in a big old-fashioned block on West 86th Street, near to Riverside Drive, was our rented apartment. The rooms were light and spacious with wonderful views both up and down the Hudson river. But almost at once we discovered the downside: nylon carpets, which charged us with static electricity every time we walked across them and gave us a shock when we touched each other – not the kind of excitement you want in the first weeks of marriage. Before we approached anything we had to first tap it with a key to earth ourselves. The central heating could not be regulated and the apartment was extremely hot. If we opened the windows a gale of black soot blew in, my first experience of how dirty Manhattan was then.

The grime of the city was not the only downside. In the mid-1960s many were depressed as the Vietnam war escalated further, and there was a general feeling of danger in New York. One night in a cab we passed two gun holdups. And when Ros, my best friend from school, who coincidentally lived nearby, and I took her children to Central Park there were streets between Broadway and the park that we avoided because of a threatening atmosphere. The park itself was ill tended, with areas where we were warned never to go. On fine days we spent more time in nearby Riverside Park watching the children in the playground while we ate lunch bought from a 'take out' coffee bar or deli. On benches near us, in an effort to banish their winter pallor, rows of elderly people sat motionless for hours with circular reflectors round their necks that allowed the weakest sun to bathe their faces.

A big bonus in our own predominately Jewish area on the West Side was Zabars, the most incredible delicatessen I had ever seen. It had an enticing salty, spicy smell, the floor was covered in sawdust and the shop was crammed with impatient shoppers. On Saturday nights you might see famous people, such as Lauren Bacall, Eli Wallach and other stars, buying good things for their weekend. Every surface was piled high with lox and smoked salmon, hunks of hot, juicy salt beef, heaps of chicken's feet, strange fish and cured meats, colourful little mountains of intriguing pickles, pastrami on rye, scallion cream cheese for spreading in milky bagels, countless other unfamiliar rye and seeded breads and cakes, and freshly made sandwiches that made a mockery of the tired English kind.

My friend Ros and her children in Riverside Park, New York City.

It was the variety and quantity of food available in Manhattan, and of the foreign restaurants and cafés, that in comparison made London seem as if it was still in the aftermath of wartime austerity, despite it being the swinging sixties. And the take-away system, known in America as 'take out' or 'to go' – still rare in England then – was speedy and efficient with the food, napkins, sauces and drinks delivered to wherever you were, if you so wished.

In what were known as the 'short order' restaurants and diners, the waiters and chefs used to shout the orders in 'diner lingo', said to date back to the late nineteenth century. This was a different language rather than shorthand; 'Burn one, take it through the garden and pin a rose on it' was simply a hamburger with lettuce, tomato and onion. 'Adam and Eve on a raft', a waiter shouted into the kitchen and two poached eggs on toast were swiftly produced, while a chef called out 'foreign entanglements' as a plate of spaghetti was ready. After a mysterious call for 'Put out the lights and cry', a plate of liver and onions was handed to a man on the next table. There were many orders for 'a blonde with sand', meaning coffee with cream and sugar, while tea was unsurprisingly 'boiled leaves'.

But what I wanted most was domestic life and cooking for my husband and friends. Almost every day I would walk to the nearest supermarket, Gristedes, at the end of our street. It was a cramped place with narrow aisles and a disorganised, grubby feel, but the variety of the stock was bewildering, as was the large size of everything, and the amount I seemed to buy – all packed into huge brown paper bags, which I struggled home with. Slightly alarming, too, were my fellow

Pumpkin and sweet potato soup

Until I went to America I didn't realise that pumpkin was edible, thinking of it only as something to be cut out as a toothy face with a candle inside it for Hallowe'en. I didn't much like pumpkin pie, but in Houston we had a delicious soup like this. Sensually smooth, rich and golden, it's a perfect lunch soup for a cold day.

Serves 10 as a starter, 8 as a lunch or supper

1kg pumpkin (about ½ medium pumpkin)

450g sweet potatoes

2 medium onions

50g butter

1.8 litres chicken stock

2 teaspoons clear honey

300ml double cream

¼ nutmeg, grated

2 rounded teaspoons caraway seeds

50g unroasted peanuts

2 tablespoons groundnut or sunflower oil

1 level teaspoon dried chilli flakes or powder

2 handfuls of coriander leaves

sea salt, black pepper

Cut the skin off the pumpkin, scrape away any seeds or stringy part and cut the flesh up roughly. Peel the sweet potatoes and cut into smallish cubes. Peel and slice the onions.

Melt the butter in a large, heavy-based saucepan over a medium heat, add the onions and fry until golden brown. Add the pumpkin, sweet potatoes and chicken stock, sprinkle with sea salt and bring to the boil. Cover the pan, lower the heat and simmer gently for 15–20 minutes until the pumpkin and sweet potatoes are really soft.

Using a blender or food processor, purée the mixture in batches, pouring the purée into a clean saucepan. Stir in the honey, cream, grated nutmeg and caraway seeds. Bring to the boil again and let bubble gently for 4–5 minutes. Remove from the heat and season with salt if needed and a little black pepper.

Roughly chop the peanuts. Heat the oil in a small frying pan over a medium heat, add the peanuts and stir around for a minute or two, then add the chilli. Stir for another minute, then take the pan off the heat. Before serving, roughly chop the coriander leaves. Throw the chilli peanuts into the soup, followed by the coriander leaves.

Potato, tomato and mascarpone bake

In Little Italy, the Italian area of New York, the food was authentic and generous at our favourite small restaurant. It was here that I first tasted the delicious combination of potatoes, tomatoes and anchovies. This is my own version – a simple recipe, which can be made ahead and kept warm in a low oven. It goes well with almost anything.

Serves 6

750g potatoes

625-750g plum tomatoes

50g tin anchovy fillets in olive oil

4 large cloves garlic

250g mascarpone

50g piece Parmesan cheese

butter for greasing

sea salt, black pepper

Heat the oven to 180°C/Gas 4. Peel the potatoes and steam or boil until cooked through but not falling apart. Let them cool slightly and then slice fairly thinly. Pierce each tomato with the tip of a sharp knife, then put them into a bowl, cover with boiling water and leave for a minute or two before draining. Now peel the tomatoes and slice fairly thickly across. Cut the anchovies across into small pieces. Peel the garlic and slice across finely.

Generously butter a large, shallow ovenproof dish. Put a layer of potato slices on the bottom, sprinkle with some of the anchovy and garlic pieces and follow with a layer of tomato slices. Continue alternating in this way, finishing with a layer of potatoes. Stir a little salt and a generous sprinkling of pepper into the mascarpone, then spread on top of the potatoes and grate the Parmesan coarsely over the top. Bake near the top of the oven for 45–60 minutes, until the top is speckled brown all over.

shoppers, mostly middle-aged women with an abrupt manner and loud guttural voices; their hair often in curlers and sometimes faces white with cracking face-packs or thick cold cream. When I asked a check-out girl, who must have recognised me from my frequent visits, if she could possibly tell me where something was, she retorted crossly, 'What do you mean, can I? It's my job isn't it.' I sometimes found myself longing for the friendliness of a London corner shop.

Back in our apartment block, I often shared the elevator with two friendly old Austrian ladies. One morning, after snow had fallen thickly overnight, I was puzzled when I heard them discussing how warm and sunny it was, until I realised they were talking about the weather in Vienna, which they had not returned to since they had escaped from the Nazi occupation and persecution of Austrian Jews in 1939. The ladies told me about a former occupant of the apartment block, the multi-talented Jack Roland Murphy, known as Murph the Surf, who only a little over two years before had been involved in the biggest jewel robbery in American history, from the nearby Museum of Natural History. 'He was very polite and seemed such a gentleman,' they said.

Meat loaf with blue cheese filling

Meat loaf, like shepherd's pie, is true comfort food and deserves a revival. Of the many versions I have experimented with, this one is my favourite. It is rich in flavour and oozing with tangy cheese.

Serves 4–5

450g lean beef or lamb mince

1 small-medium onion

100g smoked rindless streaky bacon

75g chestnut mushrooms

50g fresh brown breadcrumbs

1 rounded teaspoon dried oregano

6 tablespoons tomato ketchup

2 medium free-range eggs

100g St Agur or other blue cheese

1 tablespoon whole milk

½ level teaspoon chilli powder

butter for greasing

sea salt, black pepper

Heat the oven to 180°C/Gas 4 and butter a 1kg loaf tin. Put the mince into a large bowl. Peel the onion. Chop the onion, bacon and mushrooms finely and add to the mince. Stir in the breadcrumbs, oregano and 3 tablespoons tomato ketchup. Whisk 1 egg and stir thoroughly into the mixture, then season well with salt and black pepper. Spoon half of the mince mixture into the prepared tin and spread level.

Crumble the blue cheese into a bowl and stir in the milk. Whisk the second egg and stir thoroughly into the cheese mixture with the chilli powder. Spread the cheese mixture evenly on top of the mince in the tin. Spoon the remaining mince mixture over the cheese and level the surface. Put the tin into the centre of the oven and cook for 1 hour.

Take out the meat loaf and turn up the oven to 240°C/Gas 9. Loosen the sides of the loaf with a knife and turn out carefully onto an ovenproof serving dish. Smear the top with the remaining 3 tablespoons tomato ketchup and return to the oven for 10–15 minutes until glazed.

Let the meat loaf stand for 8–10 minutes to cool slightly before serving. Cut into thick slices with a sharp knife.

Devil's food cake

Airy, yet rich and moist, with a sharp cranberry filling to contrast the chocolate, this cake can be served for tea or as a pudding. I prefer a dusting of icing sugar to the usual coating of white American frosting.

Serves 6–8

100g dark chocolate (at least 55% cocoa solids)

3 tablespoons warm water

250g plain flour

1½ level teaspoons bicarbonate of soda

½ teaspoon baking powder

150g butter (at room temperature), plus extra for greasing

250g dark muscovado sugar

3 large free-range eggs, beaten

150ml whole milk

juice of ½ lemon

For the cranberry filling

100ml fresh orange juice

100g caster sugar

200g fresh cranberries

To finish

icing sugar for dusting

Butter two 22–24cm sandwich tins and line the bottom of each with a buttered disc of baking parchment. Break the chocolate into small pieces and put into a bowl set over a pan of very hot but not boiling water. Add the 3 tablespoons warm water and stir until the chocolate is melted and smooth. Remove the bowl from the heat and cool slightly.

Heat the oven to 180°C/Gas 4. Sift the flour, bicarbonate of soda and baking powder into a bowl and set aside. Whisk the butter in a large bowl until soft, then whisk in the muscovado sugar until fluffy. Whisk in the eggs, followed by the melted chocolate. Pour the milk into a measuring jug and stir in the lemon juice to sour the milk. Using a large metal spoon, stir the soured milk into the chocolate mixture alternately with the flour mixture.

Divide the cake mixture evenly between the tins and gently spread level. Bake just below the centre of the oven for 30–40 minutes until well risen and springy to touch in the centre.

Meanwhile, make the cranberry filling. Put the orange juice into a saucepan and stir in the caster sugar. Add the cranberries, cover the pan, bring to the boil and simmer for 5 minutes. Cool and then chill in the fridge.

When the cakes are cooked, leave them in the tins for about 10 minutes, then carefully turn them out onto a wire rack to cool. When cold, put one cake on a serving plate, spread with the cranberry filling and top with the second layer. Before serving, sift icing sugar over the top of the cake.

Since Murphy is reputed to have become a reformed character during his years in prison, was released early and then ordained as a minister, perhaps they were right. Among the world famous gems Murphy stole was the huge, honey-coloured Eagle Diamond, which has never been found. It is thought to have been broken up and sold as many separate diamonds, but the Austrian ladies told me then that they knew Murph the Surf had thrown it into the Hudson river.

During our time in New York, David had to return to Texas to work on a film he was making for the CBS series, 60 Minutes. I went with him, taking the Hasselblad camera he'd given me as a wedding present, as still photographs were needed for the film's publicity. We flew to Houston and the next morning went to film thousands of Salt Grass Trail riders coming into town at the end of their 90-mile ride from Cat Spring, Texas, an annual event to herald the Houston Livestock Show and Rodeo. The long procession of men, women and children, dressed in western cowboy style and accompanied by traditional wagons, was an extraordinary sight. But the most moving moment occurred the following day as we filmed the rodeo parade in downtown Houston.

As we watched a passing group of mounted cowboys and beauty queens, a uniformed soldier just back from Vietnam pushed through the crowd and flung his arms round one of the beauty queens, kissing her passionately. Both of them had tears streaming down their faces; the beauty queen was the soldier's wife and this was their reunion.

Having been in cosmopolitan New York, I hadn't yet experienced real American breakfasts. I've never liked eggs for breakfast but in Houston I ate fried grits, hash browns and roast beef hash. Later in the day I especially enjoyed baked corn, mustard greens and fried okra. Corn was a staple ingredient; I loved the yellow corn bread with its slightly grainy consistency, but not crumbled into sweet milk to make a drink called 'Crumblin'. There was iced tea at every meal.

With the increasing popularity of Tex-Mex dishes, there were chilli restaurants everywhere. Texans claim that the use of chilli in southern US cooking, including the famous chile con carne, originated in their state, brought to them from Spain, not next-door Mexico. Bean dishes abounded – with names like cowboy beans, red fire beans and, of course, barbecued baked beans. Black-eyed, pinto, lima and many other beans were used. They were known collectively as 'musical fruit', presumably for their notorious after-effect.

The CBS director wanted me to take some publicity stills of David dressed as a cowboy so we called in at the famous department store, Sears Roebuck, and bought a complete outfit including a $5 stetson hat. We drove to stables outside Houston where David was to ride round a field trying to look authentic. On arrival he climbed out of the car, put on his hat and then took my camera. At that moment there was a strong gust of wind and I watched in horror as his hand instinctively shot up to stop the cheap hat from flying away while simultaneously dropping my £900 Hasselblad onto the tarmac road. Luckily the expensive camera was famously strong and survived the fall.

Our most surreal experience in Texas was in the Houston Astrodome, a vast domed stadium built two years before and the largest covered football/basketball stadium in the world at that time. It was the dream of flamboyant Judge Roy Hofheinz, who called it the Eighth Wonder of the World and carpeted the field, an acre in size, with an artificial grass that he patented 'Astroturf'. We visited him in his private apartments in the dome. Guarding the entrance were two six-foot Thai dogs, carved out of teak. Roy, a large man in horn-rimmed spectacles with dark hair swept back with Brilliantine, sat behind a huge desk inlaid with black marble on a gaudy replica of the Sun King, Louis XIV's throne, smoking a long cigar. On the desk sat a gold-plated telephone with numerous extensions; no papers were visible. Three television screens were set in the opposite wall, which was 'papered' with fur.

When I asked for the bathroom I was not surprised to find that all the taps and fixtures were gold plated and that floor, walls and ceiling were covered with gold carpet, but I was slightly alarmed to find myself sitting on a gold fur lavatory seat. For the judge's personal use the apartment contained a one-lane bowling alley, a three-hole putting green, a patio with imitation orange trees, a ten-seat movie theatre and much more, all unspeakably kitsch. But the more shocked his visitors appeared to be, the more delighted the judge was. He himself slept in the Presidential Suite under the American presidential seal; only one president, Lyndon Johnson, had slept there for a night in 1965.

* * *

When our time in New York came to an end in May we heard that the legendary 1930s liner, the RMS Queen Mary, was to be retired from its transatlantic service within a few months because of the increased popularity of air travel. It seemed a unique chance to experience one of the final journeys on the glamorous ship, so we splashed out on first class tickets to enjoy it in the style for which it was known. It was worth it. The Art Deco grandeur and scale of the floating city was breathtaking, our wood-panelled cabin total luxury, and best of all, we had five days of supreme gourmet food. The first night, wearing evening dress, Captain Treasure Jones greeted us in the opulent dining hall. The room was three stories high with wide columns and a huge inlaid transatlantic map on one wall with a motorised Queen Mary slowly moving across the ocean. The stewards were mostly ageing cockneys who had worked on the liner for decades. Friendly and

informal, I recall one bringing round a large bowl of caviar for the second time and asking, 'More blackberry jam, love?' before he spooned a large dollop onto my plate. He told me that I could ask ahead for any dish I wanted, so each morning I looked through the cookbooks I had with me, chose the most skilled and expensive treat I could find, and rang the kitchens. The chefs seemed delighted by the challenges.

To work off our enormous meals we spent time in the gymnasium, where all the exercise machines were the original 1930s ones made of polished mahogany and included a simulated horse and camel. Nobody else was ever there. Long-term gym-master Don Valente (pictured right with David) was a small bald man resembling a music-hall character. As he moved us from machine to machine he told us indiscreet stories about the film stars and grandees who had come to his gym over the years; Bette Davis who never took off her sunglasses and the Archbishop of Canterbury who fell off the simulated camel, and how many of them had confided scandalous secrets. Every morning printed invitations to cocktail parties were slipped under our door, and after dinner we always danced till late. On the last night, as we walked on the empty deck looking out at the glassy calm sea lit by a full moon, we regretted that a wonderfully unreal time had to come to an end.

Baked cheesecake with a ginger crust

Only when I reached New York did I realise how luscious a baked cheesecake can be. It started me off on endless experiments – finely grated orange or lemon rind is a good addition to this one.

Serves 6–8

150g ginger biscuits

50g butter, plus extra for greasing

225g curd cheese

225g cream cheese

2 tablespoons whole milk

1 level tablespoon cornflour

75g golden caster sugar

½ level teaspoon salt

2 large free-range eggs, separated

icing sugar for dusting (optional)

Butter a loose-based 22–23cm round cake tin. Crush the biscuits in a food processor and turn into a large bowl. Melt the butter, pour onto the biscuits and stir to combine. Press evenly over the bottom of the cake tin and chill.

Heat the oven to 170°C/Gas 3. Put the cheeses into a food processor with the milk, cornflour, caster sugar, salt and egg yolks. Whiz thoroughly and turn into a bowl. In a clean bowl, whisk the egg whites with a pinch of salt to soft peaks and gently fold into the cheese mixture, using a metal spoon.

Pour the mixture onto the chilled base. Bake in the centre of the oven for 50–60 minutes or until it feels only just set to a soft touch in the centre. Leave to cool completely.

Ease a knife around the inside of the tin and then push the cheesecake up and out. Gently ease it off the base of the tin and onto a serving plate. If you like, sift a little icing sugar over the top before serving.

On St Valentine's Day 1970, having left England in the opaque grip of freezing fog, my husband David and I stepped out of the plane at Marrakech in Morocco and breathed in the caressing scent of orange blossom. I was nearly seven months pregnant with my second child. We stayed within the peach-coloured mud walls of the city at the celebrated Mamounia Hotel, decorated and furnished in a glamorous mixture of Moorish and Art Deco styles, and set in twenty acres of wonderful gardens. The hotel had accommodated statesmen, political leaders and film stars over the decades. From its opening in 1923 until the Second World War, guests would come for long periods to escape the cold of Northern Europe – often the whole winter, bringing their own furnishings. Perhaps the most well known visitor was Winston Churchill, who stayed regularly during the winters of the 1930s and painted the gardens he loved from various points, in different lights.

By the 1970s the interior of the hotel was slightly shabby but still retained the soul and romance that was lost in subsequent renovations, though the magic of the gardens has endured. Our balcony looked over an orchard of orange and lemon trees whose blossom filled our

scent of orange blossom

room with what could have been the most expensive and intense perfume. Tall palms filled the distant view, while on the other side of the building the mountains of the High Atlas could be seen sparkling in the sharp winter sun, thickly covered in snow.

Towards dusk we headed for Jemaa el Fna, the vast market square in the centre of Marrakech next to the souk's bewildering maze, packed with traditional arts and crafts, and mischievous traders trying to sell them for several times their worth. As we arrived we saw many circles of people crowding around something in their midst. These enthralled spectators were of all ages, villagers from outside Marrakech, Berber farmers from the desert and mountains, and – hard to believe now – only a few tourists. In the centre of the circles were snake charmers, performing monkeys, storytellers, fortune-tellers, scribes, healers, singers, dancers, acrobats, magicians, musicians with drums, flutes and unfamiliar stringed instruments, and even dentists. Wearing bright-coloured robes and large multi-coloured, tasselled conical hats, water sellers walked amongst the circles, carrying water in a leather bag on their shoulder and a necklace of clinking copper cups round their neck. The orange juice stalls had almost packed up, but I managed to have a glass. As I had been told, the intense fresh juice of Moroccan oranges is probably the best in the world.

As it got dark the square filled up more and more, and we noticed smoke on the other side. Walking towards it we realised that scores of kitchens and makeshift restaurants had materialised, lit by the bright white light of gas lamps. There were great copper cauldrons of soup and goat or lamb's head stews bubbling over portable gas rings, and charcoal braziers for grilling. Trestle tables were crammed with colourful salads, piled up to a neat point. Bowls of hot snails and plates of just-grilled mutton, goat, lamb's brains, merguez sausages, chicken, whole fish, aubergines and other vegetables were ready for customers who ate on benches and stools, or walked from one kitchen to another, trying something at several. Smoke and steam from the cooking often almost obscured the chefs and rose high into the black night above, illuminated against it. The scene looked like a vast stage set, a fine example of Morocco's truly exotic atmosphere. A doe-eyed little boy came up to David, as if unaware that he had his pregnant wife by his side, and asked if he would like to meet his sister, or if he preferred there was his brother. When both had been politely refused he added, 'My mother is very beautiful too.'

A day or two was spent reading and relaxing by the magnificent pool at the hotel and enjoying the wonderful food. At the Mamounia we first tried *bastilla*, or *basteeya*, the famous rich, crispy pigeon pie sprinkled with icing sugar, which is served on special occasions. The combination sounded odd: pigeon, almonds, eggs and orange flower water with icing sugar, cinnamon and saffron, but the taste and texture were sublime. I ate it greedily, using my fingers, which is the correct way, though the waiter didn't look as if he thought so. Next morning I was taken into the kitchens to see ouarka pastry, used for the pie, being made. The chefs were all women; women, rather than men are accepted as the best cooks in Morocco. Two of them were making the pastry; light as air, delicate yet crisp, ouarka is surely the king of thin layered pastries and far superior to filo. Although the ingredients – fine semolina flour, water and a spot of oil – are simple, the method is so skilled that it is hardly ever made at home. I watched as one woman with deft hands lightly spread out a ball of dough on a hot plate until it was transparently thin. The other woman then somehow put this almost invisible circle between two pieces of paper to keep it flexible. They told me that ouarka takes three months to learn how to make followed by years of regular practice. I understood why.

Ever since I had left Syria as a child I had longed to see real desert again, but first we had to cross the High Atlas mountain range by the pass of Tizi-n-Tichka. It seemed a long journey as the road twisted higher and the landscape became harsh and unwelcoming; we saw nobody else on the road and I felt slightly vulnerable in our little rented Renault 4. At Telouet Kasbah we stopped for a picnic, shivering in the icy wind. The extensive ruins of older buildings and the vast, decaying early-twentieth-century part, staffed by one thousand slaves until only fourteen years before, had belonged to the Glaoui family, known as the Lords of the Atlas, feudal chieftains of the Berber tribe. I found the place desolate and was relieved when at last we descended and saw a flat plain of rose-coloured desert open out below us.

On the road in the Atlas mountains.

We spent that night on the plain in a cold room of the partly ruined Taourirt Kasbah beside Ouarzazate. The labyrinthine fortress had been seized by the government in 1956, along with all other Glaoui properties, on the death of the family chief, Thami El Glaoui, governor of Marrakech and one of the richest men in the world. In 1970 Ouarzazate was just one street of unremarkable modern buildings next to a village of traditional mud houses and courtyards. We ate moussaka and kebabs for supper at the only place we could find on the street, a simple café run by a Greek whose father had been at one of the French

Crispy pigeon pie

This party piece – a deliciously aromatic fusion of flavours – isn't a true Moroccan bastilla, but it is inspired by those I have eaten there, and less laborious to make. Alongside I serve a green salad – with fennel slivers and coriander and mint leaves added – and a bowl of yogurt to spoon onto your plate. The filling can be made ahead.

Serves 8

12 pigeon breast fillets, skinned

350g red onions

3 large cloves garlic

generous walnut-sized piece fresh root ginger

75g unsalted butter

2 tablespoons olive oil

3 rounded teaspoons ground cinnamon

1 rounded teaspoon paprika

finely grated rind and juice of 1 lemon

2 level teaspoons caster sugar

150g blanched almonds

6 medium free-range eggs

4 tablespoons whole milk

1 rounded teaspoon turmeric

large handful of flat-leafed parsley

350g filo or strudel pastry

1 level tablespoon icing sugar

sea salt, cayenne pepper

Cut the pigeon breasts into small pieces. Peel, halve and finely slice the onions. Peel and finely chop the garlic and ginger. Melt 15g of the butter with the olive oil in a wide flameproof casserole dish or large, deep frying pan (with a lid) over a medium heat. Stir in the garlic, ginger, cinnamon and paprika, followed by the pigeon. Stir for a minute or two, then add the onions and the lemon rind and juice. Cover the pan and cook over a low heat for about 40 minutes, stirring now and then, until the pigeon is tender. Then remove the lid, stir in the sugar and bubble to reduce the juices down. Season to taste with salt and cayenne pepper and leave to cool.

Meanwhile, brown the almonds in a dry frying pan and then whiz briefly in a food processor to chop. Whisk the eggs in a bowl with the milk, turmeric and a little salt. Melt a knob of butter in a saucepan over a low heat, add the egg mixture and scramble slowly and lightly, stirring only once or twice. Remove from the heat and leave to cool. Heat the oven to 180°C/Gas 4.

Pull the leaves off the parsley stems and chop them roughly. Stir into the cooled pigeon mixture with the almonds. Melt the remaining butter. Brush a loose-based deep cake tin, about 18cm in diameter, thinly with butter. Line the tin with a sheet of filo, bringing it up the sides and allowing the excess to overhang the rim; keep the rest of the filo covered with a damp cloth so it doesn't dry out. Then lay another sheet of filo across the first one (at a 90° angle) and continue like this, buttering the sheets between each layer, and reserving two sheets.

Now spoon half the pigeon mixture into the filo-lined tin and level the surface. Spread the scrambled egg evenly on top and cover with the remaining pigeon mixture. Fold the overhanging filo over the filling and then lay the remaining filo sheets on top. Press the excess pastry down inside the edge of the tin and butter the top.

Cook the pie in the centre of the oven for about 30 minutes until well browned. Push the pie up so it is just on the tin base, then using a wide spatula, lever it carefully off the base onto an ovenproof serving plate. Put back in the oven for about 20 minutes to crisp the sides. Before serving, sift icing sugar over the top. Use a very sharp knife to cut into slices.

Foreign Legion outposts in Morocco. In the late 1980s, owing to the agreeable climate and proximity to unspoilt desert and mountain landscapes, Ourzazate became the base for several film studios and a tourist centre; it is now a modern desert city with countless luxury hotels and an airport.

The next morning, as we walked between the old village buildings before leaving, we heard a terrible screeching sound and then spotted a trickle of blood seeping slowly down a mud slope towards us. As we walked on we saw that it came from a sheep which had just had its throat slit by two men who were now starting to cut open its stomach. Nearby two others were doing the same to a black goat. A pretty little Berber girl wearing her best clothes – a pale lemon coloured robe belted with a tattered scarf and a headband embroidered with gold – watched them. We discovered that this was the beginning of Eid Al-Kabir, or Festival of Sacrifice, commemorating the Prophet Ibrahim's willingness to obey Allah's wish that he sacrifice his son Ismael. People pay tribute each year by slaughtering one of their animals and offering the meat to charity. The villagers told us that every part of the sheep and goat would be used to make tasty dishes. The meat would be cooked over a charcoal brazier in a tagine (the earthenware dish with a pointed lid that catches steam and creates delicious juices); the liver would be wrapped in caul and grilled as kebabs called *boulfaf*; there would be heart kebabs too; and the stomach and intestines would be stewed in a pot.

As we left the village and drove south, the sun shone with a clarity only found in deserts. We passed through a spectacular landscape of desert cliffs, oases with palm groves, fields of green crops, orchards of blossoming almond trees and dramatic gorges with rivers shimmering between the rocks. I can remember few more idyllic or peaceful picnic spots than those we found during that time.

On the edges of palm groves, built from the desert mud, were *ksars* – fortified villages that looked as if they had been sculpted by a giant's hands into towers of different heights and widths, making arches and crenulations, which gave each village a different silhouette. The villages were the same buff colour as the ground they were built on, making them appear as if they had grown from it, rather than been made by man. The life of the villages was internal so we were intrigued when we were invited into one by a group of men we met sitting on the stone perimeter wall of a field, all wearing white turbans and long djellabas

Spiced carrot salad with mint

It was on my first visit to Morocco that I discovered how well spices complement the sweetness of carrots. Conveniently, this salad can be made ahead. Serve it as part of a meze spread, or as a side salad.

Serves 4

350g small carrots

1 pointed red pepper

3 large cloves garlic

walnut-sized piece of fresh root ginger

juice of 1 small orange

juice of 1 lemon

2 teaspoons cider vinegar

1 rounded teaspoon paprika

1 rounded teaspoon ground coriander

3–5 pinches of chilli powder

1 level teaspoon cumin seeds

large handful of mint leaves

6 tablespoons extra virgin olive oil

sea salt, black pepper

If the tufty carrot stems are still green, leave them intact. Halve the carrots lengthways. Cut the red pepper in half, discard the seeds and stem, then chop finely. Peel the garlic and ginger and slice into very fine slivers.

Put the carrots, red pepper, garlic and ginger into a saucepan and strain in the orange and lemon juice through a sieve. Stir in the cider vinegar and spices. Cover and simmer very gently over a low heat for 6–8 minutes or until the carrots are cooked but still have a slight resistance. Remove from the heat and leave until cold.

Set aside a few small mint leaves. Chop the rest finely and stir into the carrots with the olive oil. Season to taste with salt and black pepper. Transfer the salad to a serving bowl, garnish with the reserved mint leaves and serve at room temperature.

Tizi-n-Test tagine

At Le Sanglier Qui Fume restaurant, on a hairpin bend in the Atlas mountains, Madame's chicken tagine was slightly different from others we had tasted; she added okra and plenty of her Hungarian paprika. Glossy and delicious, this is an approximation of it. It is not made in a pointed tagine, but if you have one it will look good as a serving dish. You will find preserved lemons in Middle Eastern grocers and delicatessens, though of course you may have prepared your own.

Serves 6

6 medium chicken joints

1 large red pepper

2–3 large cloves garlic

walnut-sized piece fresh root ginger

2 rounded teaspoons ground cinnamon

2 rounded teaspoons paprika

50g butter

about 900ml water

2–3 preserved lemons (depending on size)

350g fresh okra

juice of 1 lemon

1 rounded tablespoon honey

½ level teaspoon chilli powder

sea salt, black pepper

Pull the skin off the chicken joints and discard. Put the chicken into a large, heavy-based saucepan. Cut the red pepper in half, discard the seeds and stem, then slice lengthways into thin strips. Peel the garlic and ginger, slice both finely and put into the saucepan with the pepper strips, cinnamon, paprika and butter. Season with salt and black pepper.

Pour in the water, which should just cover the chicken. Put the lid on the pan and bring to the boil, then lower the heat and simmer as gently as possible for about 40–50 minutes until the chicken is cooked and tender.

Using a slotted spoon, transfer the chicken, garlic, ginger and pepper strips to a heated round serving dish, leaving the liquid in the pan. Quarter the preserved lemons, discard any pips, then place amongst the chicken. Cover the dish loosely and keep warm in a very low oven.

Trim the tops off the okra and then add to a saucepan of boiling salted water. Cook for about 3 minutes until the okra is just soft but still bright green. Drain and keep warm, on one side.

Add the lemon juice and honey to the reserved chicken cooking liquor in the pan. Bring to the boil, stirring to dissolve the honey, then boil fiercely, without stirring, for about 10 minutes until the sauce is well reduced and syrupy. Take off the heat and stir in the chilli powder.

Take the dish of chicken from the oven and stir in the cooked okra. Finally spoon the glossy sauce all over and serve at once.

(pictured right). Once within the high mud walls, we were led through seemingly endless dark narrow corridors to one of many small doors that led into the separate homes of the villagers. There was a smell of mud and dust. We sat cross-legged and were offered very sweet fresh mint tea and little goat kebabs from a low brass table. The Berber women of the family wore belted bright coloured clothes and jewellery, a welcome sight after the half-veils and shapeless grey djellabas we had seen in Marrakech. The family was friendly and curious but conversation was limited to hand gestures, one or two Arabic phrases I recalled from Syria, and the few French words they knew. When we left, a group of children followed us to the car, shrieking with excitement. That night the full moon – a crisply defined brilliant circle in the densely black sky – illuminated the oasis of Tafilalt,

packs of dogs howled in the French garrison town of Erfoud and inside me my baby kicked more energetically than ever. I looked out of our hotel window at the moonlit palm trees and desert beyond, and missed my little daughter at home.

Our way back to Marrakech took us over the Atlas by the Tizi-n-Test pass, a narrow and alarming road with endless narrow hairpin bends and terrifyingly steep slopes below. A few years before when David (who hates heights) was driving alone down the pass, his brakes failed; in low gear, he managed to get down to the flat plain unharmed but with white knuckles and heart racing. So it was with some relief that we stopped to have lunch at Le Sanglier Qui Fume. Opened during the French colonial era and run by a Hungarian woman always known as Madame, the restaurant served good French food with Hungarian touches, like paprika on the *poulet rôti*. We ate a big plate of hors d'oeuvres, some frog's legs, one Moroccan-style dish – a delicious chicken tagine with preserved lemons – finishing with *oeufs à la neige*. The garden, with a distant view of snow-capped mountains, was as unexpected as the food. It had an overgrown lawn with a murky pond where cousins (presumably) of the frogs we had eaten jumped about. Flower beds were decorated with twisted tree stumps and other strange objects, but most surprising was an assorted menagerie of animals. Some, like an eagle, a parrot and a monkey, were chained on the terrace, but rabbits bobbed up here and there, cats slunk through the foliage, dogs came up and jumped on you, and a stalk literally stalked about looking superior. A river rushed over the rocks below.

* * *

Marrakech meatballs

We came across this dish in the simplest of cafés as well as smart restaurants. The taste, as you break into the eggs and the runny yolk mingles with the gently spiced meat and juices, is wonderful. If you like, you can make the meatballs beforehand and keep them warm in a low oven, then increase the heat again shortly before adding the eggs and serving.

Serves 4

350g lean minced beef

2 large cloves garlic

25g fine semolina

1 rounded teaspoon ground coriander

1 small free-range egg

25g butter

2 tablespoons groundnut oil

1 rounded tablespoon tomato purée

1 rounded teaspoon paprika

150ml water

sea salt, black pepper

To finish:

4 medium or large free-range eggs

few coriander leaves

Heat the oven to 180°C/Gas 4. Put the mince into a bowl and pound with a pestle or wooden spoon until soft and smooth. Peel the garlic, cut up roughly and pound to a purée with a little salt, using a pestle and mortar. Add the garlic purée to the meat with the semolina, ground coriander, a generous sprinkling of black pepper and a little salt. Mix thoroughly, using a wooden spoon.

Beat the small egg lightly and work it thoroughly into the mixture. Using wet hands, form the mixture into balls, about the size of a small marble.

Melt the butter with the groundnut oil in a large frying pan over a high heat. Add the meatballs and fry, turning, just until browned all over. Transfer them to a wide, shallow casserole dish, or a tagine if you have one.

Mix the tomato purée and paprika with the water, season with a little salt and plenty of black pepper and pour over the meatballs. Cover and cook in the centre of the oven for 40–45 minutes.

When nearly ready to eat, break the eggs into the dish, spacing them out among the meatballs. Cover the dish again and put back in the oven for 8–10 minutes, only until the whites of the eggs have just set. Throw some coriander leaves over just before serving.

Morocco lured us back. In April 1974 we were once again in Marrakech, and this time met Bill Willis, the Queen Bee of the still small ex-pat community. Bill was a charismatic interior designer from Memphis, Tennessee, who had settled in Marrakech a few years before. He had designed several houses, crafted by skilled Moroccan artisans, for the rich and famous who wanted to live for part of the year in this beguilingly exotic city where every mode of lifestyle seemed possible. Bill had an attractive Southern drawl and was stunning, with piercing blue eyes, both humourous and wicked, and a mass of glossy black curls. Though often high on cocaine, he was generous and hospitable. Most nights he held a salon at his riad or traditional house in the centre of the Medina with its opulent Moorish furnishings, carved cedar ceilings, intricate fretwork screens and a roof terrace overlooking the shadowy maze of the Arab quarter. Since Bill was the only foreigner in the Medina, it seemed quite an adventure to find your way with a torch through the warren of dark, narrow corridors between high mud walls to his magical candlelit house. Under the domed ceiling of the sitting room you would meet people from the arts, high-class hippies, billionaires and other visitors to the city, while an attentive staff of beautiful young boys offered delicately made mezes to eat with your drinks, the best to me being little caramelised aubergines.

On this Moroccan trip we drove to the far south, and finally along a narrow dirt road to something I had always wanted to see: the 'Lawrence of Arabia' sand dunes and the Tuareg people who came to the market at Mhamid, the village at the start of the Sahara on the way to Timbuktoo. The Tuaregs, also known as the 'Blue People' because the indigo pigment used for their clothes comes off on their skin and stains it blue, are the principal inhabitants of the North African Sahara. They are from the same ethnic group as the Berbers but nomadic, travelling with camels and sleeping in goatskin tents erected in the desert. In Mhamid's rather diminished market we saw a few Tuaregs in traditional blue robes and black cotton turbans, the men rather than the women with black scarves covering the bottom half of their faces. Brahim, a man who lived in the village, said he would take us out to the sand dunes and we set off impulsively in our hired Renault 4.

Before long we saw some Tuareg tents and a handsome youth came running towards us, smiling broadly. He asked Brahim if we would like to meet his family. The tent was like the Bedouin ones I had seen in Syria, long and low with open sides, but more simple with no rugs on the pebbly desert floor. The boy's sister, who looked about eighteen, was ravishingly pretty, with a full long blue skirt and a jewelled headband under a black shawl. She appeared to be the mother of four little children and laughed as they climbed all over

her. A grandmother, who shyly pulled her scarf across her face as she saw us, cradled a new baby wrapped in an indigo blue cloth. The family (pictured overleaf) welcomed us into the tent and offered us sweet tea, dates, millet bread and thick camel yogurt as we sat on the hard sand floor.

It was mid-afternoon before we managed to reach the dunes, but they were all I had hoped for. They seemed to stretch to infinity. As the sun descended in the sky they became apricot coloured, their ridges, curves and ripples sharply defined and their swooping shapes increasingly sculptural as the shadows lengthened. A Tuareg boy from the tents had asked to come with us; alone in the dramatic sand wilderness, wearing a white djellaba and black scarf (pictured overleaf), he was a perfect model for my arty photographs. And he was invaluable when, as the light quickly faded on the way back, our Renault 4 (pictured above) stuck fast in a patch of fine sand. I immediately realised we had no food or water and thought of the regular number of travellers who died in the Moroccan Sahara each year, but the Tuareg boy calmly found some flat stones and we were moving again. By the time we reached Mhamid it was pitch dark; it had been a thrilling day.

At the end of our time in Morocco we met someone in Marrakech who was never at Bill Willis's starry gatherings. He was an old soldier, Field Marshal Sir Claude Auchinleck, known as The Auk (pictured right with his servant, Bashir). He was nearing his ninetieth birthday, though still tall and rather handsome, with a twinkle in his eye. We were introduced to him at the faded La Renaissance Café in the colonial French part of Marrakech where he went every morning for his coffee, and was called Le Maréchal. The Auk, whose honourable but rather chequered career had included being Commander in Chief of the Indian Army and the Middle East, was a general for longer than any other known soldier but had been at odds with Montgomery and Lord Mountbatten, and had a tense relationship with Churchill. To his men he was a soldier's soldier and they loved him; he had integrity, was modest, never pompous and hated affectation. Although he retired from the army in 1947, he still went on picnics in the foothills of the Atlas and looked over the landscape as if it was a battlefield, working out his defence strategy. He never mentioned his wife who had left him for a brother officer in 1946. We were immediately charmed by him and pleased to be invited to his flat for a drink.

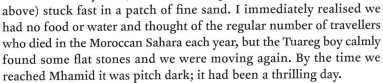

The Field Marshal's flat was more than modest, it was Spartan. There was a sitting room with a small sofa, one old armchair and a low table for drinks, with no personal objects or decorations. The Auk's bedroom contained only a narrow iron bed that looked as if it had come from ancient army supplies and a stick chair, over which his striped pyjamas and woollen dressing gown had been neatly placed by his devoted Moroccan servant, Bashir. There was plenty of gin and tonic and literally every time we took a sip the Auk asked if we would like some more, probably because he was deaf and didn't hear us politely refuse. After several drinks and on our part a shouted conversation he said, 'Now, Bashir wants to show you something.' But there was no sign of Bashir. Then, through a door on one side of the room Charlie Chaplin entered in a brown djellaba. He bowed and went out again, to be followed swiftly by Marilyn Monroe wearing the same djellaba. This was the first we knew of the Field Marshal's large collection of masks; Bashir continued to appear as De Gaulle, Winston Churchill, Mae West, Gary Cooper, Abraham Lincoln and many more, including Hitler. 'You're very honoured, you know,' said the Auk. 'He doesn't do this for everybody.'

Left: Gateway in the mud walls, Marrakech.

Almond and orange biscuits

I first tasted these little crunchy, yet gooey biscuits in Marrakech. They keep well in a tightly closed container for up to a week and make a perfect accompaniment to ice cream and stewed fruit.

Makes 25–30

50g blanched almonds

1 large free-range egg

100g icing sugar, plus extra for coating

½ teaspoon baking powder

100g fine semolina

finely grated rind of 1 small orange

a little orange flower water

oil for greasing

Heat the oven to 160°C/Gas 3. Grind the almonds in a food processor very finely. In a large bowl, whisk the egg with the icing sugar until pale. Add the baking powder, ground almonds, semolina and orange rind and mix well.

Oil a large baking sheet and have a small bowl of sifted icing sugar on one side. Wet your hands with orange flower water, then shape the mixture into balls, the size of large marbles, dipping one side of each ball into the icing sugar before placing it on the baking sheet, sugar side up. Space well apart to allow room for spreading; it is best to cook the biscuits in two batches. Keep moistening your hands with the orange flower water as you work.

Bake in the centre of the oven for 10–12 minutes; the biscuits should be the palest brown. Leave on the baking sheet for a minute or two to firm up slightly, then carefully ease off with a palette knife and cool on a rack.

THE ROAD to YAZD

At the end of 1970, when Iran was still Persia and the Shah was on the throne, Jamshed, a Persian we met in London, urged David and me to visit his country and kindly organised a trip for us. It was eight years before the revolution. Teheran horrified me with its ugly concrete buildings, noise and traffic jams, but our friend's opulent modern house on the mountain above the city was very different. Jamshed welcomed us with a bowl of the largest, most lustrous caviar we had ever seen: Caspian Beluga, its translucent pale grey pearls shimmering on a bed of crushed ice. It is second only to the finest and most rare of all, the golden Almas caviar – the most expensive food in the world. Jamshed told us that to appreciate the full magical flavour of 'the food of the gods' we should clench our fists and spoon some caviar onto the flat top half of the thumb, take it onto our tongue and carefully break the eggs against the roof of our mouth rather than swallow them whole. The taste was rich and slightly sweet but with a sea-like freshness, yet not at all salty; my mouth waters as I remember it. The only accompaniment we had was several shots of Persian vodka that made our heads spin in the cold night air when we left the house.

Two days later, at the start of our expedition, we stopped for lunch at a simple roadside café and tasted something that seemed to us almost as good as caviar. The first thing we saw as we entered the shabby room, empty of customers, was a photograph of the Shah pinned to the wall. 'My King,' said our friendly driver in a hushed and reverential voice as he bowed in front of the picture. We wondered if he really meant it. There was no menu and no choice of food. We sat down at a metal-topped table and were each given a saucer of sliced raw, sweet, onion and a plate of rice topped with a fried egg. And what rice it was: fluffy, nutty and dotted with crisped grains from the bottom of the pot. Later I learnt that the heavenly rice we ate in Iran was Domsiah, or Black Tail rice, which comes from the shores of the Caspian Sea, like the caviar. It has a distinctive aroma and is said to be so light that you can blow it away. But you wouldn't want to waste a single grain.

As we drove south we were the only car for miles on the road. The scale of the landscape rivalled the Andes seen from an aeroplane, but now we were a lone pinprick in the centre of it. And we were looking, not at huge mountains, but at a vast expanse of empty desert and distant brown hills. It was hard to believe there was a different world beyond. As we approached Isfahan, our drive across the monochrome Iranian plain made the turquoise blue tiles that covered the domes and arches of the mosques, minarets and palaces of Isfahan – gems of Islamic architecture and once the jewel in Persia's crown – seem even more dazzling. The intricate patterns of the four-hundred-year-old tiles looked almost new as they sparkled against a matching blue sky.

David reading his guidebook in the mosque. Main picture: Lone sweeper at the Shah Abbas Mosque, Isfahan.

Eggs on crispy saffron rice

This recipe was inspired by our first experience – in a roadside café – of the sublime flavour and texture of Iranian Black Tail rice, grown near the Caspian Sea. It is impossible to buy outside Iran but basmati rice is a good second best. I think this makes a perfect light lunch or supper, served with a salad.

Serves 4

250g basmati rice

2 pinches of saffron strands

300ml hot salted water

75g butter

3 pieces cinnamon stick, each about 3cm long

handful of dill

3 tablespoons olive oil

4 large free-range eggs

sea salt

finely sliced red onion to finish

Put the rice in a sieve, rinse through with water and tip into a bowl, adding 1 teaspoon salt and about 500ml water. Sprinkle the saffron strands into the 300ml hot salted water in a jug and stir around. Leave both the rice and saffron to soak for an hour or more. Then drain the rice.

Put a round, wide serving dish to warm in a low oven. Melt 50g of the butter in a heavy-based saucepan over a medium heat, add the cinnamon sticks and the rice and stir for a moment. Pour in the saffron-infused water, including the strands. Bring just to the boil, then turn down the heat as low as you can. Cover and cook for 10–12 minutes until the rice has absorbed all the liquid but still has a bite to it.

Now lay a tea-towel on top of the pan under the lid and tie the corners together on top of the lid so they don't burn. Turn up the heat as high as possible to crisp the bottom layer of rice; this takes about 8–12 minutes. Don't try to stir the rice to see if the bottom is browning, instead look at the top rim of the rice; when you see that the sides are just beginning to brown it will be ready. In my experience it has never burnt too much.

Remove the pan from the heat and leave on one side for 10 minutes, leaving the lid and tea-towel in place. Meanwhile, chop most of the dill finely, reserving a few leaves for garnish.

Fork the rice out into the warmed serving dish, scraping the crisped bottom with a fork and stirring the brown grains among the rest of the rice. Add the chopped dill and fork through, then spread the rice level.

Heat the olive oil and remaining 25g butter in a large frying pan over a medium heat and fry the eggs until the whites are set; the yolks should remain runny. Carefully transfer the eggs with a spatula onto the rice and top with a few red onion rings and the reserved dill. Eat at once.

131

The Isfahan we saw was created by Shah Abbas 1, an absolute monarch, to be his capital at the end of the sixteenth century. Brilliant, ruthless, cruel and extravagant, the Emperor needed little sleep and had a harem of hundreds of women and boys. Shah Abbas The Great, as he came to be known, was an inspired builder and rebuilt Isfahan as a place of astonishing size and grandeur, accepted as one of the most beautiful cities of the world and described in an Iranian proverb of the time as 'half the world'.

One of the things that sustained me through three days of intense sightseeing was an Isfahan speciality, a wonderful nougat called *gaz*, different from others because it included the sweet, milky sap of angebin, a plant associated with the legendary manna. Angebin was brought to Isfahan from the mountains and combined with pistachios, almond kernels, rose water and egg white to make this special delicacy. We bought it in a round cake shape and found a knife to cut it into pieces, which we quickly consumed.

Another new experience in a restaurant was a duck *fesenjan*, a rich sour and sweet dish that originated in the north of the country; the waiter said they would never serve it in summer when Isfahan becomes oven-hot, but this was December. A thick, glossy sauce made with ground walnuts and pomegranate molasses gives the dish its characteristic flavour, particularly the molasses which is made by reducing pomegranate juice to a dark, treacle-like substance with an excellent sour-sweet taste.

We also visited the poet's city Shiraz, where, for a few coins in a small post office, I bought three large primitive paintings of lively Persian scenes (one of which is shown on pages 126–7).

* * *

But despite the wonders of Isfahan, the incomparable ruins of Persepolis and the beauty of Shiraz, it is two other experiences that bring back Persia in 1970 most vividly. The first was Yazd, the stronghold of the Zoroastrians in Persia and a rival to Damascus in being described as the 'oldest city on earth'. The drive from Isfahan to Yazd took us through the most desolate, dark and forbidding desert, seemingly limitless. When we finally saw Yazd in the distance there were no shining blue domes as we had seen approaching Isfahan; the city, built entirely of mud and brick, was the same dun colour as the stark flat desert surrounding it.

In Yazd we were transported back to an earlier era; tourists were rare, and in the maze of narrow alleys, camels still walked past the smooth adobe walls and closed copper-studded doors that concealed the inner lives of the citizens of Yazd. This was a city long known for its beautiful women, but the occasional women we saw hurrying

along the alleys were completely wrapped in black chadors from head to toe, so we were unable to admire their beauty. Some of the men wore green turbans, said to indicate that they were descended from the prophet Muhammad.

Our driver led us to one of the doorways from which two besuited men emerged, apparently local government officials, and took us to see the intricately tiled Friday Mosque. The custodian, a small man wearing a white turban, gave me a chador to cover me, and later unlocked the steps to the flat cobbled roof.

From here Yazd was spread out around us, looking as it must have done for hundreds of years, with its vaulted and flat roofs, some covered with coils of dyed yarn drying in the sun – for the textile industry that once made the city famous. On almost all the rooftops were the *badgirs*, or wind towers – tall funnels which trapped every breath of wind from several directions during the baking summer heat and propelled it through hollow grooves into the rooms below – as efficient as air conditioning and much more pleasant.

Walking further along the alleys we saw a man coming towards us with what looked like a brown scarf slung over one shoulder. It was in fact *sangak*, the very long, broad and irregularly-shaped national bread of Persia, and we soon found the baker, who displayed these breads on a board outside his shop. The bread is wholewheat and sourdough,

Left: On the roof of the Friday Mosque, Yazd, David with our driver, the government officials and the custodian. Right: Me, discreetly covered for the mosque by a chador.

133

Marinated kidney kebabs

Sometimes we felt we had eaten a few too many kebabs, but in a simple café we had some particularly good kidney kebabs flavoured with sumac – the lemony flavoured red 'spice' made from the fruit of a variety of rhus plant. You can buy sumac in all Iranian and most Middle Eastern grocers.

Serves 4

12 lamb's kidneys

2 tablespoons wine vinegar

4 tablespoons whole milk yogurt

2 rounded teaspoons sumac

2 rounded teaspoons ground cinnamon

1 level teaspoon cumin seeds

2 level teaspoons cayenne pepper or chilli powder

sea salt

Cut the kidneys across into 4 equal pieces. Put into a bowl, just cover with water and stir in the wine vinegar. Leave for about an hour, then drain.

Put the yogurt into a bowl and stir in the sumac and spices. Add the kidney pieces and leave for another hour or so at cool room temperature.

Now thread the yogurt-smeared kidneys onto long, thin skewers and place in a shallow roasting pan. Spoon the remaining yogurt and spice marinade over them. Heat the grill to its highest setting.

Grill the kebabs as closely as possible to the heat for only 2–3 minutes on each side – just until slightly charred in patches and still pink in the middle.

Before serving, season the kidneys with a little sea salt and scrape all the juices in the pan on top of them – or mop them up with bread – delicious!

spongier than pita, and traditionally baked on a bed of very small hot stones, which give it a slightly dimpled look. Still warm and scattered with poppy seeds, it tasted like bread from heaven, and made us long for lunch.

In the vaulted bazaar, where many Yazd cottons and silks were sold, as well as a variety of other local crafts, we came across a small restaurant where we met the only foreigner we saw on our visit. An archetypal lone English lady traveller of a certain age, clearly intrepid and eccentric, she was being scrutinised with surprise by the locals. We were served *chelo kebab*, the well-known Persian dish of steamed saffron rice served with skewers of lamb kebabs and grilled tomatoes, which we had been told was especially good in Yazd. The lamb was certainly juicy and tender, but even more delicious to my shamefully sweet tooth was the Yazd *baghlava*, like baklava but crisper, with plenty of pistachios and the taste of real honey rather than sugar syrup. I have to admit that I couldn't help trying the rose-flavoured *pashmak*, too, a superior version of candy floss made with sesame and spun sugar, another local speciality.

* * *

Yazd honey cakes

As I have a sweet tooth, I was pleased to find that in Iran, as well as in Syria, Turkey and North Africa, I could indulge in sweetmeats infused with honey and flower water. Here I add orange for a contrasting tang. These cakes are good eaten with yogurt or luxury vanilla ice cream.

Makes about 16

225g fine semolina

50g icing sugar

100ml sunflower oil, plus extra for oiling

finely grated rind and juice of 1 orange

50g self-raising flour

½ level teaspoon baking powder

½ level teaspoon ground cinnamon

For the syrup:

100g golden caster sugar

4 tablespoons honey

5 tablespoons orange flower water

150ml water

Heat the oven to 170°C/Gas 3. Put the semolina and icing sugar into a bowl. Heat the sunflower oil in a saucepan and pour it into the bowl. Stir well and then mix in the orange rind and juice. Sift the flour with the baking powder and ground cinnamon onto the mixture and stir in.

Take up pieces of dough, about the size of a ping-pong ball, and form into short, fat sausage shapes, about 5cm long. Place slightly apart on a large oiled baking sheet. Bake in the centre of the oven for 40–50 minutes until golden and firm to a light touch.

Meanwhile, make the syrup. Put the sugar, honey, orange flower water and water into a saucepan over a low heat. Once the sugar has dissolved, increase the heat and boil rapidly for 4–5 minutes, then set aside to cool.

When the cakes are ready, lift them off the baking sheet with a spatula and place in a large shallow dish in which they fit snugly. Spoon the syrup over them and leave for several hours, basting with the extra syrup in the pan occasionally. To serve, carefully pile the cakes on a pretty plate, scraping up any remaining syrup and spooning it over. Serve warm or cold.

We were alone the next morning when we set off to see the main fire temple of the Zoroastrians, known in India as the Parsees. A group of Zoroastrian women walked past us. Chattering cheerfully in their own language, they wore patterned shawls and either embroidered dresses or baggy trousers tied tight at the ankles, a contrast to the all black figures of the Muslim women in their chadors. The fire temple was outside the city in a modern building with a shady garden. In a small room, the eternal flame flickered in a huge brass urn, as a symbol of ritual purity. Guarding the urn were two priests and there was a smell of sandalwood in the air. One priest told us that the flame had burned in Persia for 2,500 years and must not be allowed to go out, the second priest added that their god was manifested in the flame.

Zoroastrians believe in the elements of fire, water, earth and air; they do not want to pollute the earth by burying their dead, or the air by burning them, hence the two Towers of Silence just outside Yazd. Within the high circular walls on top of these man-made hills, bodies were laid out so that vultures would pick their bones clean. But recently, some Yazd inhabitants had complained that birds had been dropping pieces of human flesh onto their houses and courtyards as they flew overhead. So that year, for the first time, the dead had been buried in the ground, in concrete coffins to prevent any contamination. When we approached the two hills there were still a few birds of prey hovering above, but apparently only a few months later the familiar vultures of Yazd became extinct for lack of food.

As we walked towards the two Towers of Silence, one for men, the other for women, a man approached us. He spoke only a few words of English but pointed to the two hills, indicating that he could take

The roofs and wind towers of Yazd. Main picture: The view from one of the Zoroastrian Towers of Silence, Yazd.

Smoky aubergine with tomatoes

In Iran an aubergine purée is almost always part of a meze spread and it is usually my favourite dish. Cyrus, the wonderful cook at my local Iranian restaurant, Sufi, in west London, taught me the trick of making the walnuts we buy here, which are often dry, taste like the fresh ones I remember in Iran. If you are serving this purée as a first course, try to find some Iranian flat bread to accompany it.

Serves 4 as a first course, or 6 as an accompaniment

75g walnut halves

3 medium-large aubergines

2 medium onions

2 large cloves garlic

500g tomatoes (plum variety if available)

2 tablespoons sunflower oil

2 level teaspoons ground coriander

1 level tablespoon tomato purée

2–3 pinches of cayenne pepper or chilli powder

4 tablespoons water

2–3 tablespoons soured cream

extra virgin olive oil for drizzling

sea salt

A day in advance, put the walnut halves in a bowl and pour enough boiling water over them to cover generously. When the water has cooled, put the bowl in the fridge and leave until you need them the next day.

Heat the grill to its hottest setting. Cut the aubergines in half lengthways and grill them skin side up until the skins are blackened all over. Transfer to a board and leave to cool slightly, then scoop the flesh from the burnt skin with a metal spoon. Discard the skins and chop the flesh roughly.

Peel the onions and chop into small pieces. Peel the garlic cloves and slice across finely. Cut a small slit in each of the tomatoes, put them in a bowl and pour boiling water over them. Leave for 2 minutes or so, then drain, peel off the skin and chop the flesh.

Heat the sunflower oil in a large, deep frying pan over a medium heat, then add the chopped onions and fry until softened and well browned. Mix in the ground coriander, garlic, tomatoes, tomato purée, cayenne pepper and the water. When bubbling, stir around for a few minutes until the tomatoes soften, then add the aubergines and stir for another minute or two. Remove from the heat, season to taste with salt and leave in the pan until cold.

Shortly before eating, drain the walnuts and chop them roughly. Stir into the aubergine mixture and spoon it into a serving bowl. Just before serving, spoon the soured cream on top and drizzle a little olive oil over all.

us up one of them. We hesitated, not knowing who he was, slightly ashamed of our macabre curiosity and sensing that the towers were off limits. We looked around furtively; there was nobody in sight and the man was friendly and persuasive. At the top of the stone steps of the women's hill we came to the walls of the tower, much higher than they had appeared from below. Our new friend took us to a place where the wall had partly collapsed and we were able to clamber over to the other side. The large circular area of dusty earth was littered with human bones (pictured left) and, although the bodies were wrapped in a white cloth before being laid there, we noticed frayed scraps of patterned material. The saddest sight was a collection of small bones, clearly a child, and part of a plastic doll nearby. Two vultures circled in the sky high above us. We did not linger.

Having previously read Robert Byron's description of his visit to Firuzabad, south of Shiraz, in 1933, it was exciting to recognise from our surroundings that we were following in his footsteps, albeit by car on a bumpy dirt road rather than on horseback. Ardeshir 1, the founder of the Sassanian Empire, had built Firuzabad 1,800 years before. We drove through a beautiful gorge beside a river of such a milky blue-green hue that it could have been an illustration in a fairy story. Finally, on top of a rocky hill high above the river we saw the large ruin of the Castle of the Maiden. At the foot of the hill an odd delegation (pictured

left) was waiting for us: four soldiers in khaki, the Chief of Police in uniform, the Mayor in suit and tie, and a slightly shabby government official. After a steep climb and an exploration of the impressive structure, we were taken into the town of Firuzabad, entirely surrounded by a mud wall and a ditch, to the Governor's house, just as Robert Byron had been. The whole motley delegation, including our driver, was invited to lunch. The Governor was handsome, middle-aged and charming. Wishfully, I wondered if he could be the beautiful young son with 'oval face, black eyes and curling black lashes' of the governor who had welcomed Robert Byron thirty-seven years before.

We were very hungry by now. In a small room, everyone crowded around the table, on which was set a bowl of fresh herbs, an aubergine purée with tomatoes, some crumbled local goat's cheese and soft, thin *lavash* bread speckled with sesame seeds. Talking away animatedly, we began munching the herbs and tearing the bread to dip into the aubergine dish. Then the Governor's wife, beaming with pride, brought in a steaming earthenware pot of aromatic chicken, almonds and dried fruit with sweet sharp juices and lovely fluffy rice. We all ate very fast as the Governor said we must have enough time to see the most special sight of Firuzabad.

Astonishingly, much of The House of Fire, Ardeshir I's monumental palace, was still standing after eighteen centuries. Built with very thick walls on a gigantic scale out of un-cut local rocks and mortar, the palace has three domes; the central dome with a colossal entrance arch remains miraculously almost intact. It is thought that in the centre of this vast chamber there was a Zoroastrian fire temple. While we were marvelling, a shepherd appeared from outside and asked the mayor if we would visit the nomad school next to the palace. During the winter the Qashqai nomads come down from the mountains and pitch their tents around Firuzabad where they rear sheep and goats, make dairy produce from the milk and weave their famous carpets from the wool.

The schoolhouse was in a round white tent, but as it was a fine day the pupils sat outside in rows facing a bed-sized blackboard (pictured above), held up by a Qashqai man who crouched hidden behind it. The teacher was a pretty woman wearing a traditional headdress, many long coloured scarves, a red quilted jacket and an ankle-length voluminous skirt; her toddler stood beside her in a white bonnet, while a chicken pecked in the bare earth around their feet. Several of the little girls had light brown hair under their coloured scarves and beautiful green eyes. With our entourage we watched admiringly as a pupil was asked to demonstrate his learning on the blackboard, then we were crammed into the school tent to have tea, sitting on a brightly patterned Qashqai carpet. When we came out the teacher was still writing on the blackboard; the man holding it grinned at us. One of the children ran out and took my hand. Back in Shiraz that night I wrote in my diary that I had not wanted to leave Firuzabad.

Chicken Firuzabad with fluffy rice

This is my improvised version of a delicious dish we had for lunch at the Governor's house: aromatic chicken with fruit, almonds and delectably light rice. If you can find pomegranate molasses, do use it for its authentic sour-sweet taste and added colour.

Serves 4

250g basmati rice

2 onions

50g butter

1 tablespoon olive oil

4 medium chicken joints

50g unskinned almonds

75g dried apricots, halved

50g pitted prunes, halved

2 rounded teaspoons ground cinnamon

600ml chicken stock

1 tablespoon pomegranate molasses (optional)

sea salt, black pepper

At least an hour before you start cooking the chicken, put the rice in a sieve, rinse under running water, then turn into a bowl, add 1 tablespoon salt and cover with warm water. Leave on one side.

Peel the onions and chop fairly small. Melt 25g of the butter with the olive oil in a large flameproof casserole over a medium heat. Add the onions and stir around for several minutes until soft and browned, then remove to a plate using a slotted spoon. Keep on one side.

Turn up the heat slightly, add the chicken joints and brown well on each side. Then return the onions to the casserole and add the almonds, apricots and prunes. Sprinkle on the ground cinnamon and a generous grinding of black pepper, then pour in the stock. Put the lid on and bring to the boil, then lower the heat. Simmer very gently for 30–40 minutes until the chicken is tender.

Meanwhile, bring a fairly large saucepan of salted water up to the boil. Drain the soaked rice, add it to the boiling water and boil briskly for 4–6 minutes only; the rice should still be slightly underdone. Drain the rice into a large sieve, rinse through with running water and leave on one side.

When the chicken joints are cooked, lift them out with a slotted spatula and set aside on a plate. Then briskly boil the contents of the uncovered casserole for a few minutes, stirring now and then to prevent sticking, until the liquid is well reduced to a thick and syrupy sauce. If using pomegranate molasses, stir it in at this stage. Spoon the mixture onto the plate with the chicken. Wash out and dry the casserole dish.

Melt the remaining 25g butter gently in the clean casserole, stir in the drained par-cooked rice and arrange the chicken joints on top, spooning the thick fruit and nut sauce over each joint as you do so. Finally, cover the casserole with a tea-towel, put the lid tightly on and tie the corners of the cloth over the lid to keep them from burning. Cook over the lowest possible heat for about 20 minutes until the rice is fluffy and tender.

Forgotten cemeteries of the Raj

In 1976 my first cookery book *A Taste of Dreams* was published, so titled because in the early 1970s the demands of three young children during the day gave me no time to think what to cook for adult meals and, miraculously, I began dreaming up ideas for dishes during the only peaceful time I had – my sleep. In the winter of 1977 my friend Elizabeth, who had visited India twice, was asked to do some research on the crumbling British cemeteries by an organisation who wanted to find ways of restoring them. Elizabeth had often told me that she knew I would love India and asked me to come with her; by then I was writing food pieces for the Daily Mail and I realised that the journey would provide good copy. We left England in a blizzard of snow.

Calcutta as a first taste of India is like diving in the deep end. The mass of humanity started at the airport and when we finally pushed our way through the apparently frantic crowds to a taxi, it was dark and there seemed to be a thick warm fog. The 'fog' was in fact smoke from cow-dung cakes, a national fuel, burning on thousands of open-air fires. The smoke, mingling with dust in the air, had a particular smell that I would come to associate with arrival in India on many subsequent visits. The scene we drove through was the colour of a

sepia print and looked medieval. For miles there were rows of shops on either side of the road; they were just holes in tiny wooden shacks, lit by paraffin lamps. Groups of people squatting on the street and wrapped in tattered blankets huddled round the shops, whole families slept on the pavements, cows wandered along the middle of the road. Occasionally, strong enough to cut through the smoke, we could distinguish the potent smell of tuberoses, sold for Hindu festivals and to make garlands for weddings, as winter is the wedding season.

We were taken to the Calcutta races (pictured above) with Maurice Shellim, a doctor living in India, who was also a talented artist and author, and owned a racehorse. Bob Wright, who ran the famous Tollygunge Club, joined us; he was the life and soul of ex-pat social life in Calcutta and looked like a much larger version of David Niven. A friend from England, the photographer Derry Moore (pictured above right), who was coincidentally in Calcutta, came too. Derry was photographing old British buildings in India, of which Calcutta, the capital during the British Raj, had a wealth. I wrote in my diary that the scene around the racecourse was 'far removed from 1977' before I realised that this would apply to countless experiences in India, which

had not yet become 'the new India'. The lawns were bright green and as smooth as a golf course; stewards in starched white uniforms and Nehru caps hurried across the grass; sleek horses were paraded within white-fenced paddocks by grooms wearing neat khaki with pink or turquoise turbans that looked almost luminous when sunlight fell on them. The spectators wandered amongst the paddocks between races, or sat on white benches under the shade of the dripping tendrils of a giant banyan tree. Elegant Indian women floated across the grass in brilliantly coloured silk saris and some of the English men and women looked colonial. It was all very gracious and seemed quite unreal.

The stadium for rich spectators and horse owners was a handsome turreted building painted in white and green. In an ornate brass, white and gold lift, we were taken up to one of the private boxes on the top level. From here we could see the racecourse and the public enclosures crammed with less wealthy spectators and the Victoria Memorial, designed by Sir William Emerson in the style of the Belfast City Hall, beyond. As the horses neared the finish of a race we could hear mounting enthusiasm from the crowds in the enclosures, and at the end they all surged forward like a tidal wave and then drew back again. Those in the boxes, except for us, remained cool and reserved. Later we had tea and little cakes under umbrellas on the grass, and the sun began to sink at the start of the last race.

Fireworks heralded the Army Day party given by the Eastern Command that night. Our host was General Jack Jacob, who was from an old Jewish family in Calcutta and has been described as 'the Jewish general who beat Pakistan', referring to his success in the Indo-Pak war of 1971. An enormous white silk parachute wafted gently in the caressing breeze above the elevated circular lawn of Fort William. We were offered fruit juice, precious whisky, and warm gin and tonic. The officers were in dazzlingly smart uniform: ink blue, high-necked jackets with gold epaulettes and much braid; and skin-tight trousers with a wide red stripe down the side. The Sikh officers wore the same uniform with huge dark turbans. A very solemn Gurka band played under a red silk parachute. Beside them was a list of their repertoire, which from the handwriting style must have dated back to the 1880s. I requested 'Danny Boy', which was played slowly and mournfully, followed surprisingly by a tango. Nobody took to the floor. The General, who said he couldn't read music, nevertheless conducted the band for a time, but this didn't enliven their playing. As at the races, I felt this was not only a world away from wintry England but back at least a hundred years in time.

Dinner was our first in a private house, where you usually find the best food in India. The only drawback was that we ate very late because the men drank for hours beforehand while their wives sat, apparently contented, in rows on sofas. It was a meal worth waiting for. Puffed-up puri breads were so light you felt they might float into the air, and spinach pakora were delicately crisp, achieved by adding bicarbonate of soda to the chickpea batter and coating single spinach leaves very sparingly. New to me were *singara*, little pointed cones of the flakiest pastry filled with a delicate mixture of spiced vegetables. Mild, tender stems of lotus leaves and a soothing purée of mustard leaves were other vegetable treats. The fish cakes were particularly delicious: spiced fish bound with egg wrapped round sweet softened onions, dipped in breadcrumbs and deep-fried. Bengalis like to eat fish, mostly river fish, at every meal and a main dish was the prized hilsa fish, cooked as a curry with green chillies and mustard seed. After midnight various Bengali sweetmeats were brought in, which we miraculously managed to find room for. I loved *mishti doi*, a thick pale brown yogurt sweetened with date molasses. But there was another dish that I was told was easy to make at home, our hostesses' version of a famous rice pudding from Northern India called *kheer*, which was far more creamy and flavourful than any English rice pudding.

My friend Elizabeth photographing the old British tombs in the South Park Street Cemetery, Calcutta.

Calcutta kheer

Most people lose weight after a journey in India. I came back fatter as a result of over-indulging in the famous Bengali sweets. The markets and sweet shops in Calcutta were full of them and those I liked best were made from reduced milk, flavoured with cardamom and saffron. But these sweets are laborious to make, so I was pleased to find one that is easy – the luscious Indian rice pudding, kheer.

Serves 4

6–8 cardamom pods

550ml Jersey milk

170g evaporated milk

pinch of saffron strands

1 rounded tablespoon long-grain rice

25g flaked almonds or pistachios

1 rounded tablespoon soft light brown sugar

3–4 teaspoons rose water

Lightly crush the cardamom pods and tie up in a piece of muslin. Put this into a heavy-based saucepan with the milk, evaporated milk and saffron. Heat the milk and add the rice. Bring to the boil, then lower the heat and simmer very gently for 30–40 minutes, stirring often. Meanwhile, lightly toast the nuts.

Take out and discard the bag of cardamom. Stir the brown sugar, rose water and three-quarters of the toasted nuts into the pudding.

Pour the kheer into small individual dishes, or into one larger serving bowl. Leave to cool, then sprinkle the remaining nuts on top and refrigerate until ready to serve.

The South Park Street cemetery in Calcutta, established in 1767, was the first and most important of several colonial cemeteries we visited for Elizabeth to assess. Even though many of the tombs were seriously crumbling and invaded by weeds, with homeless families living in and amongst them, it was nevertheless a very beautiful and atmospheric place, lit almost theatrically by the sun's rays that shone through gaps in the old trees. From the branches came one of the most characteristic sounds of India, the harsh babble of countless crows; and we heard the occasional screech of a passing peacock. The vast area was a true necropolis, a maze of tombs far more grandiose than any in Europe would have been in the eighteenth and nineteenth centuries. There were massive pyramids, pavilions, statues, obelisks, urns and

Sweetbreads with ginger and chilli

Within a day or two of my arrival in Calcutta I had my first brain curry. Mildly spiced and buttery, I loved its melting smooth texture, and wanted to reproduce the dish on return. When brains became increasingly difficult to find in England I experimented with sweetbreads instead, which worked a treat. Serve with basmati rice and a mixed green salad.

Serves 4

500g lamb's sweetbreads

1 tablespoon white wine vinegar

2 fresh green or red chillies

3cm piece fresh root ginger

2 large onions

75g unsalted butter

handful of coriander leaves

sea salt

Soak the sweetbreads in cold salted water for an hour or two, changing the water once or twice to get rid of all traces of blood. For the final half hour of soaking add the wine vinegar to the water.

Meanwhile, prepare the other ingredients. Cut open the chillies under running water and discard the seeds and stems. Peel the ginger and chop finely together with the chillies. Peel the onions and slice into thin rings.

Drain the sweetbreads and pull off any skin that comes away easily. Melt 50g of the butter in a large, heavy-based frying pan and fry the onions over a fairly low heat until golden and completely soft. Add the ginger and chillies and fry, stirring, for about a minute. Then turn the heat down to as low as possible and add the remaining 25g butter. Once melted, add the drained sweetbreads and stir around. Cover and cook, stirring now and then, for 10–15 minutes.

Season to taste with a little sea salt. Transfer to a heated serving dish; if necessary you can cover the dish and keep it warm in a very low oven for up to half an hour until you are ready to eat. Just before serving, sprinkle the coriander leaves over the sweetbreads.

Cauliflower curry

It was exciting to find such a variety of vegetarian dishes in India in the 1970s, when the western world was largely meat orientated. In particular, I learnt how to transform cauliflower, by smearing florets with spices and oil and roasting them. As the main ingredient in a curry, cauliflower can be as good as chicken. If you are able to find curry leaves, add a few with the tomatoes.

Serves 4

1 medium-large cauliflower

5cm piece fresh root ginger

2 large cloves garlic

1–2 fresh red chillies

300g medium tomatoes (plum variety if available)

4 tablespoons sunflower oil

2 level teaspoons ground turmeric

2 rounded teaspoons ground coriander

1 level teaspoon cumin seeds

1 level teaspoon black onion seeds

juice of ½ lemon

juice of 1 orange

handful of coriander leaves

sea salt

Heat the oven to 160°C/Gas 3. Divide the cauliflower into smallish florets. Peel the ginger and garlic. Cut open the chillies under running water and discard the seeds and stems. Chop the ginger, garlic and chillies together finely. Cut a small slit in the tomatoes, put them in a bowl and pour boiling water over them. Leave for 2–3 minutes, then drain, peel and cut the tomatoes in half lengthways.

Heat the sunflower oil in a fairly large, heavy flameproof casserole over a low heat. Stir in the turmeric, ground coriander, cumin and onion seeds, followed by the chopped ginger, garlic and chillies. Stir over the heat for a minute, then add the cauliflower florets and stir around in the spice mixture. Take off the heat and place the halved tomatoes amongst the cauliflower. Pour in the lemon and orange juices and sprinkle with some salt.

Cover the casserole, bring up to bubbling point on the hob, then transfer to the centre of the oven and cook for 50–60 minutes. Before serving, finely chop the coriander leaves and scatter over the curry.

pagodas, as if, so far from home, people wanted to build bigger, higher and more elaborate monuments to make sure they were remembered. Kipling described the tombs as looking like 'small houses' and that the cemetery was like 'walking through the streets of a town'.

This was the final resting place, not only for many prominent people in the service of the Raj, but for countless other relatives, travellers, traders, writers, fortune-seekers and husband-seekers. Rose Aylmer, a girl of twenty, the love of the young poet Walter Savage Landor, came to Calcutta to stay with her aunt, but soon died of cholera after eating her favourite fruit, pineapple. On her black marble tomb is an elegy by the grief stricken poet which starts, 'What every virtue, every grace, Rose Aylmer, all were thine,' and ends, 'A night of memories and sighs I consecrate to thee.' We read the inscriptions on the tombs, many of which told stories of lives cut short by tropical illnesses, bravery in battle and at sea, and by impressive achievements. But as in the cemetery where my sister is buried in Damascus, the most tragic thing was to see so many graves of infants and young children. The most extraordinary tomb resembled a Hindu temple and belonged to Major-General Charles Stuart, an eccentric Irishman, nicknamed 'Hindoo Stuart'. Within a year of his arrival in India, the Irishman had become a Hindu; he bathed in the Ganges each morning and amassed a large collection of Hindu idols and deities, which were buried with him.

Mrs Wadia, a charming Parsee lady, invited us to watch dishes being prepared in her flat at the Royal Calcutta Turf Club. Her small kitchen was thick with an intoxicating smell of spices being ground under a heavy stone. An old servant in a thin white sari stood stirring milk continuously to reduce it for making ice cream. Mrs Wadia and her daughter were preparing white pumpkins and aubergines to stuff with fresh green chutney; a popular river fish called bekti was marinating in lime juice and spices, to be grilled over charcoal; a Parsee chicken dish was simmering on top of the stove.

On another evening Miss Wadia and her father Colonel Z.K. Wadia, who had a fine moustache, took us to the Bihar restaurant in New Market to try *katti kebab* – paratha bread fried on great pans with an egg pressed on each side and then rolled up with spiced chicken and onions. The rolls were luscious and the restaurant more than a stage set. Chickens pecked around our feet as we ate, the roof had fallen to the floor in some places with pieces of torn brown cloth looped across the holes, there was hardly an inch of space between the crowds, and innumerable beggars pushed their way through.

Afterwards we escaped to the comparative peace of the Hooghly river. Miss Wadia explained that it was the festival of Saraswati, the Goddess of Learning, and this was the night people would bring

A young boy's grave in the South Park Street Cemetery.

goddesses they had made and worshipped to the holy river. As we came to some steps down to the water the calm was shattered by angry shouting and drumming, and we found a large group of people having great difficulty attempting to manoeuvre a huge goddess into the water. Countless other smaller goddesses began to arrive, each with their own attendants and drumming band, as well as dancers and boys with flaming sticks. There were goddesses in swans, goddesses in elaborate houses with gardens, goddesses in boats, all made with immense care. Many sank when they were lowered into the water but others floated downstream, creating a surreal sight. Finally the huge goddess reached the river and there was a great cheer; her red-lipped white face seemed to calmly smile up at us as she disappeared into the dark water.

The Ganges from the old fort at Chunar, where we ate our picnic.

*****

Perhaps the most thought-provoking experience of our long journey was when Elizabeth and I visited Chunar, on a wide and beautiful part of the Ganges south of Benares. We had come to see an old British cemetery but first went to the top of the vast and ancient fort to admire the spectacular view of the sacred river and eat the picnic we had been given. The Ganges looked blue from here instead of the usual mud brown; music and voices floated up to us from ferryboats carrying crowds of people and wedding bands; and pigs and groups of camels walked along the sandy shore. In our stainless steel Tiffin tin we found light vegetable samosas in the top tray, below a sauce to go with them made from mint leaves, lemon juice, spices and chilli, and in a lower tray *rasgullas* and *jelebis* for a sweet element.

Until independence in 1947 Chunar was the home of thousands of Anglo-Indians. I learnt for the first time then that Anglo-Indian does not mean British families who lived in India, but the descendents of one British parent, almost always the father, and an Indian one. They were clever and hardworking but not accepted by either the British or

Potatoes with ginger and spices

Although I'd had all sorts of good potatoes in Peru, it wasn't until my first visit to India that I realised how well they go with spices. Now I often do them like this, even to accompany a Sunday roast. They are also good eaten at room temperature, drizzled with a little olive oil.

Serves 4–5

750g Charlotte or other waxy potatoes

2 large cloves garlic

3cm piece fresh root ginger

2 tablespoons groundnut oil

25g butter

2 level teaspoons ground cinnamon

3 level teaspoons ground coriander

1 rounded teaspoon ground turmeric

½ level teaspoon chilli powder

4 level teaspoons cumin seeds

large handful of coriander leaves

sea salt

Cut the unpeeled potatoes roughly into 2cm cubes and then steam or boil them until only just cooked through; drain well. Peel the garlic and ginger and chop finely together.

Heat the groundnut oil and butter in a large frying pan or a wok over a medium-low heat. Add the garlic and ginger and stir around for not more than 2 minutes; don't let the garlic burn. Then add all the spices, including the whole cumin seeds, and stir for another minute.

Next add the cooked potatoes and sauté over a medium heat for 6–8 minutes. Stir in a sprinkling of crushed sea salt, then turn into a heated serving dish. Roughly chop the coriander leaves and scatter over the potatoes. Eat as soon as you can.

Indian communities, and married amongst themselves. The English style cottages with names like Honeysuckle Cottage, Sunnyside and Bellevue stretched for as far as we could see around the old English church, but many were in ruins, and of the huge Anglo-Indian community, only six people were left. Behind the cemetery was a gigantic red brick house, clearly in a state of serious decay (pictured right); a stained marble plaque above the door read Hardless Hall. The owner was an old man, shrunk almost to a skeleton, wearing a greatcoat over striped pyjamas and three more layers of clothing. 'My name is Dick,' he said with a mischievous smile, holding out a tiny bony hand.

Decades before, Richard Hardless (pictured right) had been a handwriting expert whose skills won an important legal case for the Nizam of Hyderabad, reputed in the 1930s and '40s to be the richest man in the world. As a reward, the Nizam built the Hardless family a palace with hundreds of marble-floored rooms and a ballroom-sized central room, which they could never have afforded to keep up. Now Dick and his daughter Marie, a lively thirty-seven year old of slightly faded beauty, lived in only two of the rooms, with about four sticks of rickety furniture; everywhere else was empty, and thick with dust and pigeon droppings. Goats and chickens wandered in and out of the rotting house, and cooking was on charcoal in the dust outside.

Next door, dwarfed by Hardless Hall, was a neatly painted cottage named Cresswell Lodge, where we met an endearing elderly couple. Mr Clements, wearing a solar topee, insisted we had tea with them. We sat in their front room, furnished totally in English style with a baby grand piano on which were framed photographs of relatives in England, where they had never been. Mrs Clements poured tea into bone-china cups out of a floral china teapot and said what a good thing it was that she had made a Victoria sponge cake that morning. Before the sun went down, the Clements and Richard Hardless took us to see the cemetery of Anglo-Indian graves, and earlier ones of British soldiers and railway workers who rarely married the Indian women they lived with, and whose children started a long line of Anglo-Indians. Inscriptions were often poignant: 'In memory of Edward Harris – mourned by Nancy, a native woman, his true and faithful companion for twenty-five years.' The little group beside us, the last ones left, said nothing, and we sensed an intense atmosphere of loss.

155

Rich red quail curry

Elizabeth, Derry and I were given a lift across country from Lucknow to Agra by a group of men who were going shooting. We all squashed together in a small van for the long journey. As the conversation in India invariably turns to food they talked about how their wives cooked the game they shot – quails, partridge, duck and more. Back in England, I tried combining game birds with Indian spices and found it opened up delicious new ways of cooking them.

Serves 6

2–3 fresh red chillies

1 large red pepper

3 large cloves garlic

2 medium onions

75g butter

1 rounded teaspoon ground cinnamon

½ level teaspoon ground cloves

1 rounded teaspoon ground coriander

½ tablespoon tamarind paste

300ml very hot water

400g tin chopped tomatoes

1 tablespoon tomato purée

seeds from 3 cardamom pods, roughly crushed

6 quails

4–5 tablespoons whole milk yogurt

sea salt

Cut open the chillies under running water and discard the seeds and stems. Cut open the red pepper, discard the seeds and stem and chop roughly. Peel the garlic and onions and chop roughly. Put these prepared ingredients into a food processor and whiz to a smooth purée.

Heat the oven to 160°C/Gas 3. Melt the butter in a large flameproof casserole over a low heat. Add the ground spices and stir around for a minute, then add the vegetable purée, cover the dish and leave over a very low heat for about 8 minutes. Meanwhile, put the tamarind paste into a measuring jug, add the hot water and stir to dissolve the paste.

Stir the tamarind water, chopped tomatoes, tomato purée and crushed cardamom seeds into the purée in the casserole and season with a little sea salt.

Put the quails into the dish, cover and increase the heat to medium. When the sauce is just bubbling, transfer the dish to the centre of the oven. Cook for 1¼–1½ hours until the quails are tender enough to come away easily from the bone.

Before serving, spoon the yogurt on top of the curry, but don't stir it in.

Scenes from our Devon life, painted on the headboard of our bed at Blackberry Cottage by my friend Christina Gascoigne.

Village
of
plums

In the southwest of England, two miles upriver from Dartmouth, the River Dart swells to a mile wide at the village of Dittisham, known by locals as Dit'sum. The Dimbleby family had been taking holidays there for several years before I married David. They had an old bungalow at the water's edge with a breathtaking view and a large, steep plum orchard behind, but by 1977 David and I had three young children, his brothers had also started families and his sister was soon to follow. The bungalow simply wouldn't take all of us.

So when the old lady who lived next door died, David and I bought the dilapidated property along with its orchard, which was densely overgrown with brambles that obscured the river view. The brambles were torn away by a bulldozer, revealing a few surviving plum and apple trees. I added a quince, a medlar, a mulberry, a breed of grafted apple called Family Tree, on which cooking apples and dessert apples grew happily together, as well as blackcurrant canes, wild strawberry plants and gooseberry bushes. Before long, the making of fruit puddings, pies, tarts, ice creams, jams and jellies dominated my Devon life. And when the few remaining brambles bore large, juicy fruit, we decided to re-name the cottage Blackberry Cottage.

Eric and Trevor, the village builders, got to work and a year later we had an extended cottage that slept ten, a level terrace and lawn above the orchard, and a magnificent view of the river with beech woods and hills opposite. I spent most of the children's school holidays at Blackberry Cottage, after which it continued to be an important part of my life for more than twenty years.

Trip boats that motored up and down the river between Dartmouth and Totnes announced as they passed Dittisham that the village was 'famous for its plums'. The variety in our orchard and everyone else's was – and still is – unique to the village, but nobody is sure how it got there. One theory is that some crates of plums or prunes were salvaged when a trading ship was wrecked on its way upriver several centuries ago and the villagers planted the stones. The ship probably came from Germany, as the plums are known as Plowman, which sounds like *pflaume* (German for plum); they are also similar to a German variety called Fluegel. In this country the Victoria plum is the nearest thing, but Dittisham plums have deep scarlet juices and a more intense taste when cooked, so they make exceptionally good jam and compotes.

The linchpin of our Devon life was David's mother Dilys, a lively, loving grandmother, who retired with Ron, her second husband, to a house that also overlooked the river. We were in and out every day; the children constantly because of the fun they had with Mimi, as they called their grandmother, and because she had an unending supply of treats. The holidays were a happy ritual of boat and sailing life, river and beach picnics, annual events like Dittisham Village Day with races and games, the Easter egg hunt, the Old Gaffers' Race in which David sailed his lovely gaff-rigged boat Rocket (pictured left, pages 166 and 169), and Dartmouth Regatta.

Friends and relations came to stay, the children played with their cousins, and every evening there were large noisy meals at Blackberry Cottage. Food and the enjoyment of it – and for me cooking – was a crucial part of all we did. Every week I went to Dartmouth market where you could buy local produce of all kinds, and left staggering under the weight of enormous bags packed with food for a large household, once or twice in tears from domestic exhaustion.

Two old ladies from a Dartmoor farm ran my favourite stall, which sold butter, clotted cream and cheese. I discovered that beneath their table, hidden under a cloth, they had a limited amount of home-made farm butter. It ranged in colour from bright yellow to orange, according to the state of the grass, and had tiny pockets of water inside. With its rich, slightly cheesy flavour, it was wonderful on granary bread with cheese and good pickle. Luckily I became one of the privileged clients the ladies would sell their butter to. Even then I was only allowed to buy one packet at a time, except on the rare occasions they would let me have two.

I particularly loved Easter in Devon. Being the start of spring and a prelude to summer, it was the time of year with much to look forward to. Early spring can be cold and grey but, magically, almost every Easter morning throughout the years at Blackberry Cottage was blessed by warm sunshine, so we could put Easter eggs on the terrace table overlooking the river and have breakfast outside. At that time the high banks of the lanes were full of violets and our orchard was a carpet of primroses, so violets and primroses were used to decorate the table. Since they were edible flowers I also used them in Easter food, including a salad with primroses at lunch.

The Easter cake (pictured right) was a sharp lemon sponge to counteract all the chocolate, with pale lemon icing covered with freshly picked primroses, little nests of chocolate eggs and a chick amongst the flowers. As the children grew older, clues for the Easter egg hunt became more complex and it could extend over the entire village; but it would always culminate in our orchard with David as The Easter Egg Man, running manically up and down in a straw hat with a wide curved brim full of tiny chocolate eggs, which flew out as he ran and fell amongst the primroses, to be grabbed by anyone who got to them first.

Primrose salad

This is the salad I used to prepare when the orchard was full of primroses. During the summer holidays I'd use nasturtiums instead.

Serves 6–8

100g baby spinach leaves

1 plump head of chicory

12 young primrose leaves

2 tablespoons raspberry or cider vinegar

½ teaspoon runny honey

4 tablespoons walnut oil

16-20 primrose flowers

sea salt, black pepper

Tear the spinach leaves roughly, or leave them whole if they are very small. Cut the base off the chicory and slice across fairly thickly.

In a salad bowl (glass looks prettiest), mix the sliced spinach and chicory leaves with the primrose leaves.

For the dressing, whisk the vinegar, honey and walnut oil together in a cup and season with crushed sea salt and black pepper.

Lightly toss the salad with the dressing just before serving, scattering the primrose flowers over the top to finish.

Marinated mackerel

We were frequently inundated with mackerel, caught from the boat. With those we could not grill and eat immediately, I often made this dish – a sort of ceviche – so the fish would keep a bit longer. We now know that we should eat oily fish regularly and if you have access to really fresh mackerel there are few nicer ways to do so.

Serves 4–6 as a starter or as part of a cold lunch

500g fresh mackerel fillets, skinned

about 300ml sherry vinegar

2 large cloves garlic

good handful of flat-leafed parsley leaves

60ml sunflower oil

100ml extra virgin olive oil

sea salt, black pepper

Using a small, sharp knife, cut the mackerel into thin strips and lay in a shallow dish. Pour enough sherry vinegar over to just submerge the fish. Cover the dish with cling film and leave in the fridge for 2 hours or more.

Peel and roughly chop the garlic, then pound to a purée with a little salt using a pestle and mortar. Chop the parsley leaves fairly coarsely. Put the puréed garlic into a bowl with the two oils, season with crushed sea salt and plenty of pepper and mix thoroughly, then stir in the chopped parsley.

Remove the mackerel strips from the vinegar, rinse under cold water and pat dry, then lay in a shallow serving dish. Spoon the oil, garlic and parsley mixture over them, to coat thoroughly. Cover and refrigerate for 24 hours.

Remove from the fridge and uncover an hour before eating, to return to room temperature. Serve with sourdough or rye bread to mop up the juices.

Almost every day during the summer holidays when the children were very young we went in a motorboat we called Plum, later replaced by Rocket, upriver and along the coast beyond Dartmouth to one of the coves with a beach, taking a picnic. English seaside picnics, prone to cool breezes, benefit hugely if there is an element of warm food. Baps stuffed with grated cheese, slivered onions and herbs, wrapped in foil and heated in the oven, were the nearest I got to sandwiches. I found if I wrapped the foil parcel thickly in newspaper the baps would still be warm and lusciously gooey when we reached the beach. Hot quiches packed with vegetables and herbs were similarly wrapped. The picnic was carried on and off the boat, then into the rubber dinghy from which we had to leap onto the beach before waves submerged us; somehow it always seemed to arrive intact. This happened with babies in carrycots too, though they weren't wrapped in newspaper.

Often we cooked on the beaches, which were invariably empty in the early years when they were only accessible by boat. Everyone was sent to collect sticks or driftwood for a fire and on a very large grill

Chicken in the orchard pie

Chicken pie is popular with both adults and children, so I often made this one in Devon, using local Scrumpy cider and apples from the orchard. I usually prepared it ahead to the stage where I had put the uncooked pastry on top, then kept it in the fridge. So when we came back from a day out, all I needed to do was to glaze the pastry and put the pie in the oven. You don't really need potatoes, just a green vegetable or a salad.

Serves 6-8

10 boned chicken thighs

25g butter

1 rounded tablespoon plain flour

300ml dry cider

2 rounded teaspoons wholegrain mustard

small handful of tarragon

75g chestnut mushrooms

1 dessert apple

150ml double cream

1 medium free-range egg

375g packet puff pastry (preferably the all-butter kind)

sea salt, black pepper

Heat the oven to 180°C/Gas 4. Remove the skin from the chicken and cut each thigh into 3 pieces. Gently melt the butter in a flameproof casserole and remove from the heat. Add the chicken pieces to the casserole and stir to coat with the butter, then stir in the flour, using a wooden spoon. Gradually stir in the cider.

Put the casserole back over the heat and stir until the liquid bubbles and thickens. Now add the mustard and season with salt and plenty of black pepper. Cover the casserole and cook in the centre of the oven for 1 hour.

In the meantime, pull the leaves off the tarragon stalks and chop them roughly. Slice the mushrooms across thinly. Peel the apple, cut out the core and then cut into small chunks.

When you remove the casserole from the oven, stir in the cream, chopped tarragon, mushrooms and apple. Transfer the mixture to a 1.2−1.4 litre pie dish or similar ovenproof dish. Set aside until cold.

Whisk the egg lightly in a small bowl. Cut off a smallish piece of pastry and roll it into a couple of long strips. Brush the rim of the pie dish with egg, lay the pastry strips on top, pressing the joins together, and lightly press down onto the rim.

Roll out the pastry until it is slightly bigger all round than the top of the pie dish. Trim away the excess pastry round the edges. Roll out the trimmings and cut out shapes to decorate the pie (I can manage an apple tree, sometimes even a chicken). Cut 2 small holes near the centre to allow steam to escape. Refrigerate at this stage if preparing ahead.

When ready to cook the pie, heat the oven to 200°C/Gas 6. Brush the pastry all over with egg and cook in the centre of the oven for 20−25 minutes until the pastry is puffed and rich golden brown. Turn down the heat to 150°C/Gas 2 and bake for a further 20−25 minutes. Serve hot.

over red-hot embers we would cook excellent local sausages and sometimes mackerel, line-caught from the boat on the way. The children chased each other with long stems of fat brown seaweed; we rested in the sun and swam in the sea; some went sailing and I often climbed up the cliff and picked sea cabbage or broccoli to cook as a vegetable that night. On the way back we would moor at Dartmouth to buy ice creams topped thickly with clotted cream from the Castle Dairy. As we moved off, the children, in ecstasy, would have pools of melted ice cream moving slowly down the front of their lifejackets.

Other regular picnics were at what we called 'Picnic Point', an idyllic spot upriver by boat under majestically tall beech trees opposite the old boathouse of Sharpham House, a Palladian mansion, which loomed on the crest of the hill. On a promontory, before anyone could remember, someone had made a place for a fire with a surround of stones. It was encircled by mossy banks and fallen trees to sit on, and roofed by a high beech canopy, which kept us dry and enabled the fire to survive even when it rained. Best of all were 'night picnics'. As soon as the children were old enough to stay up we would board the boat well before sunset and motor up towards Totnes. In all weathers the River Dart is stunning for its entire length from high on Dartmoor to the sea, but on a fine summer's evening the stretch between Dittisham and Sharpham was breathtaking. The glassy water could look almost black; along the banks the branches of the beech trees touched by the salty high tide were like a neatly cut fringe; in other places velvety green fields curved gracefully down to the water's edge. Beyond Dittisham the only buildings were occasional country houses and farms so that you could imagine yourselves to have been transported back to the eighteenth or nineteenth century. Oyster-catchers and sandpipers pecked along the shingly beaches at the water's edge, cormorants stood proudly on rocks, whole colonies of herons took over trees opposite Picnic Point, while buzzards and sparrow hawks glided in the thermals high above.

Our night picnics sometimes upgraded from sausages and mackerel to pre-marinated lamb chops and best of all, a rib joint of aged Devon beef. I found I could cook rare beef – crisp on the outside and with the bonus of wood-smoke flavour – by grilling it on the big rack I used on the beach, balancing it on the stones surrounding the fire. Samphire grew by the shore, so I boiled some up to serve as a vegetable. By the time we had indulged greedily, drank quite a lot of Scrumpy, and filled ourselves with fruit and KitKats, it would be dark and time for ghost

Plum parfait

Every August, great clusters of fruit weighed down the branches of the plum trees in our orchard, and this was when I made my parfait ice cream, a great favourite. As it is so difficult to source Dittisham plums outside Devon, I have used Victorias here and added more lemon juice to intensify their flavour; if you can add a few damsons, it will be even better.

Serves 6–8

For the plums:

450g Victoria plums (not too ripe)

juice of 1 lemon

175g caster sugar

For the ice cream:

2 large free-range egg whites

pinch of salt

200g golden caster sugar

6 tablespoons strained lemon juice

300ml whipping cream

2–3 tablespoons plum or other fruit liqueur (optional)

Halve and stone the plums and put them into a saucepan with the lemon juice and caster sugar. Cover and place over a fairly low heat, stirring often until the sugar has dissolved, then continue to cook gently until mushy. Turn into a food processor, whiz to a rough purée and leave until cold.

For the ice cream, whisk the egg whites in a large, clean bowl with the salt, using an electric whisk, until they begin to stand in soft peaks. Put the caster sugar into a saucepan with the lemon juice and stir over a low heat until dissolved. Then increase the heat and boil fiercely, without stirring, for 3 minutes. Immediately pour the syrup onto the egg whites in a thin stream, whisking all the time and continue to whisk until the mixture is thick and looks like uncooked meringue.

In a separate bowl, whisk the cream until thick but not stiff. Then, using a metal spoon, gently but thoroughly fold it into the egg white mixture, followed by the plum purée, and fruit liqueur if using. Finally, turn into a serving bowl and freeze for at least 5 hours before eating.

stories. We built up the fire again and sat round telling or inventing tales, inspired by our eerie surroundings. Lit by firelight the children's eyes grew wider and finally, so they would not feel too frightened on the way home, we told them to pretend to be ghosts themselves. As they ran through the trees, they wailed at any passing boat.

Sometimes we spent Christmas in Devon and a local farmer would fatten up a goose for us. One Christmas my brother Ben, who inherited both my father's eccentricity and his passion for fireworks, came to stay. Liza and Henry, our eldest children, had reached the age of doubt about Father Christmas. But Kate, the youngest, still believed in him passionately. On Christmas Eve she was so excited she couldn't get to sleep, so at 2am Ben, even though he is six-foot-five and rake thin, volunteered to dress up as Father Christmas and deliver the stockings. The only costume we could find was David's bright red sailing oilskins

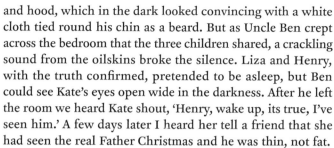

and hood, which in the dark looked convincing with a white cloth tied round his chin as a beard. But as Uncle Ben crept across the bedroom that the three children shared, a crackling sound from the oilskins broke the silence. Liza and Henry, with the truth confirmed, pretended to be asleep, but Ben could see Kate's eyes open wide in the darkness. After he left the room we heard Kate shout, 'Henry, wake up, its true, I've seen him.' A few days later I heard her tell a friend that she had seen the real Father Christmas and he was thin, not fat.

My *pièce de résistance* was my Christmas pudding. Packed with dried fruits and nuts, which I varied each year, it needed no added sugar. It was round in Dickensian style, as I cooked it in a Chinese rice steamer, and I served it on a favourite Wedgwood plate that had belonged to my grandmother. One Christmas, after we had feasted on goose, I turned out my pudding, steaming and aromatic, onto its plate, and poured brandy round it. Ben turned out the lights and lit the brandy for me. As I proudly approached the table with my flaming round pudding, there was a loud bang and the pudding exploded. The shock made me drop the precious plate, which smashed on the floor. Before lighting the brandy, Ben had deftly inserted a small firework into the centre of my pudding which, when ignited, shot pieces of it all over the room and onto the ceiling, where they stuck. I rarely lose my temper but this grand finale was too much. I lost my Christmas cheer and shouted so loudly at Ben that everyone looked frightened.

As well as the mackerel we caught from the boat, when we were prepared to get muddy, we collected large, sweet orange mussels and fat cockles from a mud bank that appeared in the middle of the widest part of the river at very low tides. The old china sink in the original kitchen of the cottage where we kept piles of sailing apparatus, oilskins, lifejackets, a jumble of canvas shoes, gumboots, buckets, spades and crabbing lines for the children, was often full of soaking mussels.

Trevor, the builder, used to take Henry fishing in his boat out at sea; if they were lucky he would bring back a bass. One late afternoon we were sitting on the lawn outside the cottage when we saw Henry coming through the gate at the bottom of the orchard after a day's fishing. He was beaming with pride and had something that looked like a long grey rag over his shoulder. It turned out to be an enormous conger eel (pictured left), as tall as Henry at thirteen and so big that much of it had to be stored in neighbours' freezers. That night I made the best steaks into a mild conger eel curry with coconut milk, green chillies, sweet red peppers and cardamom pods.

Regatta cassoulet

This was our sustenance at the annual Dartmouth Regatta evening festivities. It is full of flavour with a soothing consistency – perfect for outside eating or a winter meal. I usually made it ahead, then reheated it just before we left for the regatta and kept it hot in a huge, wide old thermos. If you want to save time you can use those good Spanish jars of large flageolet beans, but home-soaked beans are that much better.

Serves 8–10

500g dried flageolet beans

3 large onions

6–8 large cloves garlic

2 large red peppers

2 large fennel bulbs

25g butter

5 tablespoons olive oil

1.5kg stewing pork

500–600g kabanos sausages

2–3 tender rosemary stems

2 rounded teaspoons fennel seeds

400g tin chopped tomatoes

2 tablespoons tomato purée

600ml dry cider

coarsely grated rind and juice of 1 large orange

sea salt, black pepper

Put the beans into a large bowl, pour on plenty of cold water and leave to soak in a cool place until the next day.

Drain the beans, tip them into a saucepan and cover generously with water. Bring to the boil and cook at a rolling boil for a few minutes, then lower the heat. Cover and simmer gently for 20–35 minutes until the beans are just soft but not breaking up. Drain and leave on one side.

Peel the onions and cut up roughly. Peel the garlic cloves and slice crossways. Halve the peppers lengthways, discard the core and seeds, then slice across fairly thinly. Trim, halve and quarter the fennel bulbs.

Melt the butter with 2 tablespoons olive oil in a wide, deep frying pan over a fairly high heat. Add the onions and cook, stirring, until well browned. Add the garlic and stir for a minute, then tip the mixture into a large bowl. Heat another 1 tablespoon oil in the pan and fry the peppers until beginning to soften, then add to the onions and garlic with the fennel.

Cut the pork into chunks and slice the kabanos sausages roughly into 3cm lengths. Heat the remaining 2 tablespoons olive oil in the pan over a high heat. Fry the pork in batches, just enough to brown them all over, then add to the bowl along with the sliced sausages.

Heat the oven to 230°C/Gas 8. Tip the cooked beans into a very large casserole and add the contents of the bowl together with any fat from the pan. Strip the rosemary needles from their stems and add to the casserole with the fennel seeds, tinned tomatoes, tomato purée, cider and orange rind and juice. Stir with a wooden spoon to mix all the ingredients together, seasoning generously with sea salt and black pepper.

Cover and cook in the oven for about 20 minutes, until the juices are just bubbling, then lower the setting to 140°C/Gas 1 and cook for a further 2½–3 hours, stirring once or twice. Check the seasoning before serving.

The annual Dartmouth Regatta at the end of August was a splendid finish to the summer holidays. In the late afternoon we would moor in the harbour to watch the Red Arrows as they swooped from behind the steep hills on one side of the water to the other, their rainbow-coloured trails criss-crossing what, miraculously, was almost always a clear blue sky. Later, as it grew dark, we had a perfect view of the spectacular fireworks above the ancient town. Nobody spoke much on the dark journey back upstream; adults drank the remaining wine or some whiskey and tired chidren shivered in the night air, finally almost sleepwalking along the lane to their beds in Blackberry Cottage.

Blackberry Cottage tart

I was inspired to make this tart because the blackberries from the few surviving brambles in our orchard turned out to be so large and juicy.

Serves 6–8

For the lemon pastry:

175g strong white bread flour

50g golden caster sugar

100g butter

finely grated rind and juice of 1 lemon

For the filling:

300ml soured cream

500g large blackberries

4 tablespoons blackberry or blackcurrant jelly

1 tablespoon lemon juice

To make the pastry, sift the flour and sugar into a bowl and make a well in the middle. Gently melt the butter in a saucepan over a low heat with the grated lemon rind and juice, then pour into the flour mixture and mix thoroughly with a wooden spoon until you have a smooth dough.

Using your hands, press the warm dough over the bottom and up the sides of a 24–25cm loose-based flan tin to line it, pressing a rolling pin over the top to neaten the edge. Lightly prick the base of the pastry with a fork and chill in the fridge for at least 30 minutes.

Heat the oven to 200°C/Gas 6. Lay a piece of baking parchment in the pastry case, fill with dried beans or rice, and bake blind in the centre of the oven for 20–25 minutes until the edges are pale golden. Remove the paper and beans. Pour the soured cream into the pastry case and bake for 10 minutes. Place the tart tin on a wire rack and leave to cool completely.

No longer than 2 hours before eating, arrange the blackberries on the tart. Warm the jelly with the lemon juice in a pan over a low heat, stirring until smooth, then slowly spoon it over the berries. Leave until the jelly is cold.

To unmould, carefully push up the base to release the tart from the side of the tin. Now, using a thin metal spatula, ease the tart off the base onto a large serving plate; if you find this difficult, just keep it on the base. Leave in a cool place, but not the fridge, until ready to eat.

a meeting in Rangoon

The car that met us at Rangoon airport on the last day of January 1981 was a 1946 Humber in an advanced state of decay. I had been travelling in India with David and my friends Elizabeth and Tobias, and reached Burma from Calcutta. Of the few cars we saw, and the buildings, none could have dated from later than 1948. I noticed that a large 1940s clock on a British clock tower had stopped and wondered if the hands had been in the same position since January 1948, when British rule ended and Burma became independent.

In early 1981 General Ne Win was still President. Having seized power in a military coup d'état in 1962, he founded the 'Burmese Way to Socialism', the start of a downward spiral in the economy and increasing deprivations and isolation for the Burmese people, which continue to this day. The maximum tourist visa then was for seven days, which allowed only a tantalising glimpse of this fascinating and beautiful country, and its delightful people. Naturally kind and gentle, eager for any contact with a world beyond theirs, and still smiling despite their continuing hardships under a self-serving regime that provides nothing for them, these endearing people left an intense impression on me and I have returned to Burma several times since.

The day after we arrived was my birthday. It started with a cup of green tea made with large leaves from high up in the mountains of the Shan States, far better than any I had tasted before, with no trace of bitterness. For breakfast we were offered Burma's most famous dish, Mohingar – a fish broth with fat rice noodles, which have a mildly fermented taste. Almost everyone eats Mohingar for breakfast and it is also served in homes, restaurants and from street stalls throughout the day and evening, with variations. River, lake or seawater fish – all of which are excellent in Burma – are added to the noodles and broth, with lemon grass, garlic, ginger, shrimp paste and roasted chillies. Other inclusions might be banana stems, fried onions, hard-boiled eggs, gourd fritters, lentil powder, coriander leaves and other leafy herbs. It is a comforting dish at any time.

Sustained by Burma's national dish, we made for its famous national monument, the Shwedagon pagoda (pictured right) in the centre of Rangoon. On our way through streets with hardly any traffic, we passed crumbling colonial houses and stalls selling steaming Mohingar, cooked on braziers. The ancient shrine of Shwedagon, which began as a legend and became history, is said to hold at its core eight hairs of the Buddha. The main bell-shaped dome or stupa of this iconic place of worship and pilgrimage – one hundred metres high and encased in many layers of pure gold leaf – can be seen from all over Rangoon. Even today, if you arrive by air at night and look below, it shines out from the barely lit streets and dark buildings of the capital.

The Shwedagon's gold changes throughout the day from a sharp, shimmering sparkle in the midday sun to a rich glow when the sky turns rosy as evening approaches. The top part of the stupa is solid gold. Above it is a single seventy-six-carat diamond on an orb studded with many thousands of diamonds, rubies, sapphires and other gems, so large that they can be seen glinting from ground level. I watched the expressions on the faces of the visiting Burmese pilgrims, most of them incredibly poor, as they stared up in awe at the wealth of gold and priceless jewels. I wished I knew what they were thinking, but the atmosphere was happy. Amongst hundreds of other small gold stupas and temples, families walked around as if on an enjoyable day out, some stopping to pray now and then. Children ran about excitedly and played games, while groups of novice monks in their rust-red robes sat on temple steps laughing and chatting.

I had an introduction to a Burmese authoress, Daw Mi Mi Khaing, who had published a book on cooking and entertaining 'in the Burmese way'. Mi Mi Khaing was now old and almost blind but nevertheless invited us to dinner at her house in Rangoon. During the summer she lived in the cooler Shan States with her husband, Sao Sai Mong,

Burmese fish curry

On more recent visits to Burma we have had time for a few days rest on the idyllic and so far unspoilt Ngapali beach. There are many little restaurants behind the beach, run by families who live in shacks at the back of them. They serve fresh and skilfully cooked fish, seafood and vegetable dishes. One of our favourite dishes is a fish curry, which they tell you is cooked 'in the Burmese way', with tomatoes. Barracuda is often used, but any firm white fish will do. Serve with basmati rice, cooked in coconut milk if you have a tin handy.

Serves 6

2 fresh red chillies

400g ripe medium tomatoes

5cm piece fresh root ginger

4 large cloves garlic

1 medium-large onion

5 tablespoons groundnut oil, plus extra for frying

2 rounded teaspoons ground turmeric

1kg firm-fleshed white fish fillet, skinned

1 rounded teaspoon soft brown sugar

2 tablespoons fish sauce

300ml water

juice of 1 lemon

bunch of spring onions

Cut open the chillies under running water, discard the seeds and stems, then chop the flesh finely. Pierce each tomato with the tip of a sharp knife, then put them into a bowl, cover with boiling water and leave for a minute or two before draining. Peel the tomatoes and chop the flesh fairly small. Peel the ginger and garlic and chop finely together. Peel the onion and chop finely.

In a large bowl, mix 3 tablespoons of the groundnut oil with the turmeric. Slice the fish into large chunks, add to the bowl and rub all over with the oil and turmeric mixture. Heat a thin film of oil in a large frying pan over a high heat. When it is smoking, add the pieces of fish and fry for a minute only on each side, turning them gently. Remove from the heat and set aside.

Pour any remaining turmeric-infused oil from the bowl into a flameproof casserole. Add the remaining groundnut oil and place over a medium heat. Add the onion and stir over the heat until soft and browned, then add the ginger and garlic and stir around for a minute or two. Add the tomatoes and chillies and cook, stirring, for about 5 minutes until the tomatoes are mushy. Stir in the sugar, fish sauce, water and lemon juice. Take off the heat.

Add the fish carefully, so as not to break up the pieces, and pour in any remaining pan juices. Cover the casserole and set over the lowest possible heat – the juices should barely bubble. Cook for 10–15 minutes, depending on the thickness of the fish, until it is just cooked.

Meanwhile, slice the spring onions across into 5cm pieces, using as much of the green part as you can. When the fish is ready, add the spring onions, cover again and cook for another 2 minutes. Serve at once.

Spiced cauliflower with eggs

Cauliflowers are plentiful in markets all over Burma and they are typically cooked in healthy and delicious ways. I ate something like this almost every day while travelling in Burma. Once the ingredients are prepared and ready, this dish can be on the table in minutes.

Serves 4 as a side dish

500g cauliflower florets

walnut-sized piece fresh root ginger

3 large cloves garlic

100ml hot water

2 rounded teaspoons ground turmeric

juice of ½ lemon

1 tablespoon fish sauce

2 tablespoons groundnut oil

2 rounded teaspoons sesame seeds

½–1 level teaspoon chilli powder, or 1 rounded teaspoon chilli flakes

2 large free-range eggs

handful of coriander leaves

sea salt

Slice the cauliflower florets thinly. Peel the ginger and garlic and slice both into the thinnest possible slivers.

Pour the hot water into a measuring jug, stir in the turmeric, then add the lemon juice and fish sauce.

Heat the groundnut oil in a wok over a medium heat, then add the sliced cauliflower and stir around for a minute or two until it begins to soften; it should still have a bite.

Now add the ginger, garlic and sesame seeds and continue stirring for another 1–2 minutes. Pour in the turmeric liquid and add the chilli and a sprinkling of salt. Stir over the heat for another minute or two.

Lightly whisk the eggs in a bowl and pour into the cauliflower mixture, stirring around briskly for a minute or so until the egg scrambles in strands.

Turn the mixture into a heated serving bowl. Tear or chop the coriander leaves roughly, scatter over the cauliflower and eat at once.

a Shan prince said to be charming and elegant. It was winter now, though to us Rangoon felt hot and humid. Daw Mi Mi welcomed us into her small colonial house. She was petite and still had black hair, a sharp intelligence and real panache. She talked about Burmese food and family customs, and explained that rice is the fundamental part of every meal; other dishes are to make it more palatable and varied.

The rice Daw Mi Mi served that evening was cooked in coconut milk with fried onions. A tender duck curry made in the Burmese way with fish sauce and lots of garlic and onions was served with it. We also had our first taste of butterfish; smeared with coconut cream, chopped ginger and spices, then steamed in banana leaves, it was a real winner. There were some excellent Burmese salads too: intensely sweet little tomatoes with a chopped roasted peanut dressing; smoky grilled aubergine mashed with chopped raw onion and green peppers;

grated green papaya with lime; and a delicate white seaweed salad. Pickled tea leaves (pictured right) featured in a famous salad, and a pressed catfish and tamarind relish was intriguing too. Somehow we still had room for a rich semolina pudding made with creamy coconut milk and topped with crunchy poppy seeds. Finally, as at most Burmese meals, we ended by eating lumps of palm sugar, like strong-flavoured fudge, which is said to help digestion.

As our visa gave us so little time, we had been advised to fly to Pagan and Mandalay, but we were determined to have a railway journey, as a better way of seeing and experiencing the country. An experience it certainly was. We left Rangoon at 7am, sitting on wooden seats that were not as uncomfortable as you might imagine. The old British narrow-gauge track made the carriages rock with a rhythmic sound, which at first was quite comforting. And, as the speed was not great, we were able to take in our passing surroundings, particularly as there was no glass in the windows.

A large group of very young novice monks in our carriage ran up and down, laughing, eating and playing games with marbles on the floor. Each time we stopped, rows of pretty young women came up to the windows with baskets on their heads, piled high with fruits, salad leaves and tasty vegetable snacks fried in a dry, light tempura batter (pictured right). We bought their snacks and drank sweet Burmese tea made with condensed milk, which was surprisingly refreshing.

After rocking about on the wooden seats for nearly twelve hours we were relieved to be told that we would reach Mandalay in less than an hour. A moment later there was a loud noise and the train stopped abruptly, throwing us around. The conductor told us that insurgents on the line ahead had derailed the train. Apparently, I exclaimed in surprise, 'What do you mean, surgeons on the line?' We didn't see any insurgents, but we sat in the carriage or walked in the dark outside for six hours until the train driver and various people who had appeared from nowhere got us on the rails again. Finally, at nearly 3am, we reached Mandalay and were taken by horse and cart through empty streets to a hotel.

The next morning, on the ferry across the river to Sagaing, David smoked his first Burmese cheroot (pictured right). It was almost white on the outside, eight inches long and very thick, with a filter made of corn husks. The pale dried leaf of a local shrub encased crushed tobacco mixed with soft wood pieces seasoned with tamarind pulp, local alcohol and aniseed. Although very different to his favourite Havana cigars, David seemed to quite enjoy it.

Slow-cooked pork with pumpkin

The largest pig I have ever seen was in Burma; she was over six feet long, about half as wide, and had seven tiny piglets, each one no bigger than their mother's nose. You see pigs wherever you go and pork is often cooked at home in stews and hotpots. This is a memory of a comforting, flavourful dish we enjoyed in 1981. The flavour is better still if you cook the dish the day before and reheat it. Rather than use preparation-intensive tamarind pods, buy a jar of smooth tamarind purée, available in Asian shops and some supermarkets.

Serves 4

2 large onions

4 large cloves garlic

walnut-sized piece fresh root ginger

750g boneless pork

3 level teaspoons soft brown sugar

300g piece skinned, deseeded pumpkin

2 tablespoons groundnut oil

1 level teaspoon chilli powder

1 rounded teaspoon ground turmeric

300ml water

2 tablespoons dark soy sauce

2 tablespoons tamarind purée

1 rounded tablespoon peanut butter

large handful of coriander leaves

Peel, quarter and thinly slice the onions. Peel the garlic and chop finely. Peel the ginger and slice into thin slivers. Cut the pork into 3cm pieces and sprinkle all over with the sugar. Slice the pumpkin flesh into roughly equal-sized pieces.

Heat 1 tablespoon of the groundnut oil in a fairly large flameproof casserole over a medium heat. Add the sugared pork and stir around quickly until browned all over, then remove the pork and leave on one side.

Heat the remaining tablespoon of oil in the casserole, add the onions and cook, stirring, until soft and richly browned. Now stir in the garlic, ginger, chilli powder and turmeric and cook, stirring, for another minute. Remove from the heat, return the pork to the dish and add the pieces of pumpkin.

Heat the oven to 150°C/Gas 2. Measure the water in a jug and stir in the soy sauce, tamarind purée and peanut butter. Pour into the casserole dish, stir and cover. Bring up to bubbling on top of the stove and then place on a low shelf in the oven for 2–2½ hours until the pork is very tender.

Taste for seasoning and add more chilli and a little more soy sauce if needed. Before serving, roughly chop the coriander leaves and stir them into the dish.

Sagaing is a concentrated centre of Buddhism. A steep hill and its surroundings are closely covered with over five hundred monasteries and nunneries, all painted white, which dazzle in the sunlight and house about six thousand monks and nuns. We were taken to a monastery, which was also an orphanage for about eight hundred young boys, who had school lessons for part of the day and Buddhist teaching for the remainder. Most of the boys' parents had either been killed in border skirmishes, or were too poor to feed them. Taken in as novice monks, they were waiting for their lunch in a large hall when we arrived. Shaven-headed in their robes, they squatted on the floor at low tables in silence, with their hands clasped in prayer.

It was a moving scene; clearly the older boys looked after the little ones in a brotherly way and tried to replace some of the parental affection they had lost. The food – a bowl of rice each, with little pots of curry – was donated by different private benefactors each day, and cooked in the monastery.

The ruins of Ava (pictured right), once an ancient city and capital of the Burmese kingdom for four hundred years, occupy a sort of peninsula on the Irrawaddy river near Mandalay. Today Ava is firmly on the tourist track and drivers of uncomfortable horse-drawn carts clamour to take you around. In 1981 it was a magically peaceful place with hundreds of ruined pagodas, overgrown with creepers and flowering plants, dotted amongst lush fields of crops. In the centre of brilliant green rice fields, which were once the royal rice fields, was the most beautiful teak monastery. We wandered around its hundreds of teak pillars and perfectly preserved carvings, the silence broken only by a group of little urchin boys. The endearing boys had found old clay pipes in the earth and tentatively asked if we'd like to buy some, which we happily did.

Lying loose on the floor or in stone niches in the crumbling pagodas, were many perfect little buddhas; it was hard to believe that nobody had thought to pocket them. As we left, the sun was setting over the Irrawaddy, the best moment. Two bullock carts were collecting water in the shallow part near the bank. The water turned a deeper orange by the second and the bullocks, carts and their drivers, smoking large cheroots, were sharply silhouetted against it.

Even during the winter months when there is far less water in the Irrawaddy, its vast width is breathtaking. At some points it can look like an infinitesimal lake, which is how it appeared on our journey by local boat from Mandalay to Mingun. We had clambered into a long narrow wooden boat, packed with families carrying large baskets of market shopping. The only foreigners, we perched tightly together on narrow benches, large and ungainly amongst the petite, graceful Burmese, yet surrounded by warm smiles and feeling extremely welcome.

Rice noodles, chicken and vegetables

Lunch on our first trip to Burma was almost always a quick bowl of noodles from a stall or simple restaurant, with varying ingredients. Back in England I found they were also perfect for a nutritious and quick light lunch or supper.

Serves 4

250g flat rice noodles

4 large chicken thighs, boned and skinned

1–2 fresh red chillies

350g carrots

3cm piece fresh root ginger

2 large cloves garlic

75g unsalted peanuts

2 tablespoons groundnut oil

100g bean sprouts

2 tablespoons fish sauce

1 tablespoon rice vinegar

2 good handfuls of baby spinach leaves

handful of coriander leaves

Cook the rice noodles according to the packet instructions, drain and leave on one side.

Slice the chicken thighs into fairly thin slivers. Cut the chillies in half lengthways under running water and discard the seeds and stems, then slice crossways as thinly as you can. Peel the carrots and slice finely, on a slight slant. Peel the ginger and garlic and chop together finely. Chop the peanuts roughly.

Heat the groundnut oil in a large wok over a medium heat. Add the ginger and garlic, sliced chillies and chopped peanuts and stir around for a minute. Then add the chicken slivers and stir for 3–4 minutes until the chicken is opaque. Now add the carrot slices and bean sprouts and stir for another minute or so, to soften the carrots slightly.

Add the cooked noodles, fish sauce and rice vinegar and toss until the noodles are reheated. Throw in the spinach leaves and stir briefly, just until wilted. Turn into a heated serving bowl. Scatter the coriander leaves over the noodles and serve at once.

Moonlight bananas

At a little family-run restaurant called Moonlight, lit only by tiny candles and a necklace of miniature coloured lights garlanding a large pot plant, we were once given – as an extra to our meal – bananas cooked in coconut with a hint of lime. The bananas in Burma are far better than any we get here so I have added a little cardamom and salt to enhance the dish. All over Asia, salt is often added to coconut milk in sweet things – it really brings out the flavours.

Serves 4-6

6 small bananas

1 lime

50g golden caster sugar

400ml tin coconut milk

½ level teaspoon salt

seeds of 4 cardamom pods, finely ground

Heat the oven to 170°C/Gas 3. Peel the bananas, slice in half crossways and put into a bowl. Grate the rind from the lime in fine strips, using a zester if you have one; put on one side. Squeeze the juice into a cup, stir in the sugar and then pour onto the bananas, turning them with a wooden spoon so they are well coated. Arrange the banana pieces in a fairly shallow ovenproof dish, such as a 23–24cm round flan dish, in which they fit in a single layer with a little room to spare.

Tip the coconut milk into a bowl and whisk with a fork until smooth, adding the salt and cardamom. Stir in the lime rind and then pour the milk over the bananas. Cover the dish with foil and cook on the centre shelf of the oven for 25–35 minutes until the bananas are very soft.

Serve the bananas either warm or at room temperature.

The nearer you get to Mingun the less you can believe in the size of the unfinished pagoda that King Bodawpaya started to build in 1790, using thousands of slaves. Cracked almost in half by an earthquake in 1838, the immense ruin dwarfs other white pagodas around it, yet it was planned to be three times higher, the largest building in the world. The King abandoned the project in 1797, most probably because it was proving too costly. When our boat reached the shore we could not resist the snacks being taken round on wide plates balanced on the sellers' heads. There were small fish, all sorts of vegetables and bean curd, briefly deep-fried in the lightest, crispiest batter. Snacks like these and bowls of noodles in a light broth – with chicken or fish, vegetables and coriander leaves – had become our favourite lunch.

Sometimes we were fortunate enough to find Shan noodles – flat white noodles made from a type of sticky rice, which are the best of all. There was a feeling of quiet calm as we sat eating on the bank of the Irrawaddy at Mingun. Beside us a woman appeared to be washing a shallow wooden bowl in the muddy river water until we noticed that amongst the mud in the bowl were tiny glinting specks. She was panning for gold.

The women and children's faces were painted with thanaka (pictured right), a cream-coloured paste made from the powdered wood of a mature perennial tree with a similar scent to sandalwood. Thanaka is used both as a cosmetic and for protection. It promotes a clear, smooth complexion, can be shaped on the face to enhance features, and is often painted in intricate leafy patterns. The prettiest girls clearly take great trouble each day when they apply their thanaka. Yet it's also cooling to the skin, an antiseptic, and guards against sunburn and insect bites.

The village, which has since been moved by the government, was still amongst the thousands of unrestored ancient temples of Pagan at the start of the 1980s. Our time in this romantic setting was too short and I vowed to return. In 2007 I did and was relieved to find that despite the changes at Bagan, as it is called now, the sight of the temples – stretching as far as the eye can see – is still sensational. They cover an extraordinary 16 square miles from the eastern bank of the Irrawaddy. This time my friend Johnny and I made friends with a horse-and-cart driver, Myaing, who took us to lesser-known temples where few tourists went. He talked tenderly to Ninyo, his old, thin white horse as we clip-clopped along. Two years later we took Myaing some presents and he insisted we should come to meet his family, promising that his wife would cook us something 'very delicious'.

In the softness of early evening he took us in the cart to his house – a roofed platform on stilts with a palm leaf roof and panelled walls of woven bamboo. To one side under an awning lived Myaing's beloved horse. There was no furniture in the house and the family slept on mats on the floor. Only one corner, where babies were born, was partitioned off. The kitchen consisted of an open wood fire and some blackened pots and pans. Waiting for us was Myaing's pretty wife, their four children, a grandfather (who had escaped the Japanese during the war by hiding in a temple), several neighbours and a splendid feast.

A makeshift table of planks was covered with countless little bowls containing crispy little fish from the river, spicy coated chicken legs, creamy yellow beans, tomatoes with dried shrimp and fresh peas, things they called 'gooseberries' which were sharp and covered with crushed peanuts and chilli, and more. There was no electricity and we ate by the light of the thin candles you find everywhere in Burma, that burn down in minutes. It all tasted very good indeed, but best of all was the warm atmosphere. Lit by the light of the spluttering little candles was a circle of faces that my mind's eye always sees now when I think of Burma: beauty, gentleness and open smiles, always smiles.

mint–infused hotpots and morning glory

Broadening my perspective of life is one of the things I love most about travelling, as well as being able to escape briefly from my own concerns. In 1992, after twenty-five years of marriage, David and I separated, so in February 1993 I was especially glad to be going on a distracting far-off trip. My travelling companion was my old friend Elizabeth, and we had chosen Vietnam, which had just opened its doors to tourists, though we were told that once in the country we would need written government permission to stay overnight anywhere.

We started from the palatial splendour of Government House, Hong Kong, staying with Chris Patten, who five years later was to oversee the handover of Hong Kong to the People's Republic of China, and his wife Lavender. The evening before leaving for Vietnam, I started to run a bath, then crossed the vast bedroom to choose something to wear. After a few minutes I turned to see water flowing swiftly through the bedroom and out into the corridor beyond. In no time, eight servants in crisp white uniforms with red piping appeared, to turn off the flow and mop up. The water was already leaking through cracks in the floorboards into the formal dining room below. I was mortified and apologised profusely to the Pattens. 'Don't worry at all,' said the last governor, 'it's good *feng-shui*.' I felt that my luck might change ...

The dilapidated Hotel Majestic in Saigon was a very different scene. At least our room had a fine view of the Mekong River, on which boats lit with necklaces of fairy lights busied to and fro. The air conditioning in the hotel sounded like an ancient factory, keeping us awake throughout the first night and doing little to cool the humid heat. Breakfast on the hotel roof the next morning cheered us up. As we looked down at the lively activity beside and on the river, we were surprised by excellent croissants – our first experience of one of the legacies of French Indo-China.

That morning, with an interpreter who spoke fluent Russian but few words of English, we plunged into Saigon's roofed market, which was dominated by women. Jars of vegetables and shrimps of all sizes in brine were beautifully arranged. And there were all kinds of salted fish; large conical piles with countless varieties of dried shrimp and the same of rice; and shiningly fresh fish, including beautiful soft-shell crabs and crayfish. Succulent morning glory and perky salad leaves looked as if they had been picked just five minutes earlier. The many different types of bean curd and noodles intrigued me, as did the little banana leaf parcels of raw salted beef left for ten days to mature.

Steamed squid with a ginger and chilli dipping sauce

We ate this simple but perfect quick dish for lunch in a café overlooking the white sands of China Beach near Hue. Vietnamese seafood is incredibly sweet and succulent. To make this dish taste almost as good as it does in Vietnam, cook the squid very briefly to keep it tender, and add a little sugar.

Serves 4

900g ready-prepared small squid with tentacles

good handful of mint leaves

2 rounded teaspoons black peppercorns

2 level teaspoons coarsely ground sea salt

2 level teaspoons caster sugar

For the dipping sauce:

1 fresh red chilli

walnut-sized piece fresh root ginger

1 clove garlic

4 tablespoons rice vinegar

3 teaspoons fish sauce

Put a large serving bowl in a low oven to warm. Slice the squid pouches thinly across into rings, leaving the tentacles whole; set aside.

For the dipping sauce, cut the chilli open lengthways under running water and discard the seeds and stem. Peel the ginger and garlic and then chop them, together with the chilli, very finely. Tip into a small shallow serving dish and add the rice vinegar and fish sauce, stirring to combine.

Now chop the mint leaves fairly small; put to one side. Crush the black peppercorns and sea salt together coarsely, using a pestle and mortar.

Just before serving, pour some water into the bottom of a large, wide steamer and bring to a fierce boil. (Or you could use two smaller steamers.) Once boiling, put the squid in the steamer basket and set it over the water. Cover tightly and steam for a minute, or two at the most, until the squid just turns opaque.

Immediately turn the squid into a bowl and sprinkle in the caster sugar, pepper and sea salt, and the chopped mint. Toss to mix, then pile into the warmed serving bowl.

Serve at once, with the dipping sauce alongside for everyone to dip their forkfuls of squid into.

Beyond the market was a school where cooking – as well as sewing, hair cutting and swimming – were taught to people of both sexes, all ages and every occupation. The building was open plan with low divisions. In one space, a group of students learning how to kill crabs and cook them with ginger and spring onions was being eyed by another group having their hair washed and cut. On the opposite side, next to a sewing class, a lesson was in progress on boning a chicken and stuffing it with mushrooms, ham and pork fat, but also fresh coconut and soaked dried shrimps. The result was a sort of cross-cultural French galantine, with the chicken's head sewn on, so it stayed upright, looking like a live but featherless bird.

The French culinary legacy was strongly evident everywhere. Each morning in Vietnam, even in remote villages, we saw freshly baked French baguettes for sale (pictured above). The crusty bread was often spread with a coarse liver pâté, which had a typical French country-style flavour but was sprinkled with slivers of red chilli, coriander leaves, slices of spicy fish cake and *nuoc nam*, or fish sauce – the seasoning made from fermented anchovies which characterises so much Vietnamese and other Asian food. Unexpectedly, the mixture tasted exceptionally good. We found other charcuterie (pictured left),  including pork pâtés, brawns and large sausages, which were often wrapped and cooked in banana leaves. There were also beef *daubes*, *civets*, *ragoûts*, *potages* and French-style cheeses, all with Vietnamese names sounding much like the French ones, and a mixture of provincial French and Asian flavourings. In the open air French-style cafés strong black coffee was served – percolated through aluminium coffee filters on the cups exactly as in France, only here another more recent influence crept in; the French filters were made from scraps of metal from American aircraft left after the Vietnam war.

When a Vietnamese girl was to marry, we were told, she had to prepare a meal for her future mother-in-law to show that she was a good cook; if she proved not to be after the marriage it caused an angry rift between the two families. Vietnamese families make any occasion a reason for a feast: marriage; the birth or death of a family member; the completion of exams; even a baby having reached a month old; as well as each anniversary of these happenings. The anniversary of a death calls for two feasts, one the day before the anniversary and one on the actual day to call the soul of the dead person back. The dishes served must be ones the deceased relative liked.

In Giac Lam Pagoda, one of the oldest temples in Saigon, we came across a cheerful funeral feast (pictured right). The deceased's relatives looked happy and the tables were laid with a tempting array of vegetable dishes. A large group of saffron-robed monks were already tucking in voraciously at the table in the centre, where they had just conducted the funeral service. A shaft of smoky sunlight highlighted the largest of them. There was a wonderfully happy, irreverent atmosphere; noisy children ran about everywhere and the relatives laughed, smoked and chatted loudly, inviting us to come and eat with them. It was like a lively restaurant in a temple. To one side an old fortune-teller sat, looking in a book and writing out advice for the single relatives on when they should get married.

Hue, the ancient imperial capital until 1945, when the last emperor Bao Dai abdicated, is set around the Perfume River in central Vietnam. Many of the old imperial buildings in the area of the citadel, including the emperor's palace, have been destroyed – either during the fighting between the French and Viet Minh in 1947, or bombed by the Americans during the Tet Offensive of 1968 – but it remains a beautiful place. In 1993 there were few tourists and only one hotel, the Perfume River Palace Hotel, a shabby monstrosity built by the Americans during the Vietnam War and later 'orientalised' in astonishing kitsch. However, it had a wide view of the great river and the flat-bottomed wooden sampans (pictured right); these housed large families and each boat had its own temple built on the awnings. Beyond was the riverside market, a sea of conical straw hats amongst a wealth of produce.

195

Chicken noodle hotpot with coconut milk and fresh leaves

On our journey in Vietnam we had all sorts of hotpots, which were really more like soups with plenty of added ingredients – pork, chicken, fish and/or seafood, vegetables and herbs, with or without coconut milk. For this one-pot meal, I have used a combination of chicken and seafood. It's perfect for lunch or a light supper.

Serves 4

125g thin wheat noodles

2 fresh red chillies

large piece fresh root ginger

3 large cloves garlic

3 free-range boneless chicken breasts, skinned

1 litre chicken stock

50g coconut milk powder mixed with 3 tablespoons water, or 100ml coconut cream

juice of 1 lemon

several handfuls of mixed leaves (including baby spinach and plenty of mint)

2 tablespoons groundnut oil

250g bean sprouts

125g cooked, peeled prawns, with tails intact

generous handful of coriander leaves

sea salt

Cook the noodles in boiling salted water until they are just soft, then drain in a sieve, rinse with cold water to stop the cooking process, and set aside.

Cut the chillies in half lengthways under running water and discard the seeds and stems, then slice across finely. Peel the ginger and garlic, cut into small pieces and then into very thin slivers. Slice the chicken breasts across thinly.

In a saucepan, bring the chicken stock to the boil, then remove from the heat, add the coconut milk paste or coconut cream and lemon juice and stir together thoroughly.

Combine the salad leaves and mint in a serving bowl; set aside.

Heat the groundnut oil in a flameproof casserole over a fairly high heat, then add the sliced ginger, garlic and chicken. Stir around briskly for about 2 minutes. Add the sliced chillies and bean sprouts, and continue to cook, stirring, for a further 1–2 minutes until the bean sprouts are just limp.

Now pour in the stock mixture and stir in the cooked noodles. Bring up to bubbling, then remove from the heat and add the prawns. Taste and add a little salt if needed. Finally, scatter the coriander leaves into the dish.

Put the bowl of salad leaves and mint on the table, along with the hotpot. To serve, ladle the hotpot into warmed soup bowls and encourage guests to throw leaves into their individual portions.

Our twenty-two-year-old guide, Tue, spoke charmingly idiomatic English learnt by listening to the BBC World Service. 'My father sees the world through rose-coloured spectacles,' he declared. We wondered what he meant as he informed us that his father had worked for the Americans at Hue, and was interred for three years after the war ended in 1975. We never met Tue's father but we called in on his grandfather who lived in an old French house surrounded by mango, lychee and Chinese apple trees. The old man, looking like a mandarin with a long wispy beard, welcomed us. In the front room were two wooden bedsteads with straw mats instead of mattresses, and a coffin. Tue told us that a few years earlier his grandfather thought he was dying and ordered his coffin. As he didn't die the coffin remained in readiness.

An elderly servant brought us cups of fragrant green tea from the primitive kitchen (pictured left) – simply a mud floor with two blackened cooking pots balanced on stones over smouldering logs. Chickens strutted around or perched on a shelf between some bananas and vegetables. Tue's mother, Vinh, was waiting for us at their house nearby; she was serene, rather beautiful in a sad way, and for some time talked about the terrible experience of the Vietnam War, during which both her parents had been killed. Then she collected herself and fetched us some skilfully constructed little boxes of fresh banana leaves that encased delicious mixtures of sticky rice, coconut, sweet bean and banana. And, since it was lunchtime, she swiftly cooked a wonderful mixture of vegetables over her wood fire.

We had seen few guests in the hotel but one night, as we sat in the rooftop bar, we heard a fanfare of music and a procession of thirty-nine American men and women dressed in mandarin costumes, some of them aged between eighty and ninety, came into the room accompanied by Vietnamese officials. They passed us, looking straight ahead, and entered a room next door to sit at a long dining table. Later we discovered from the Americans that they belonged to an organisation in Kansas City founded by President Eisenhower 'to enhance understanding between people of different countries and cultures'. Apparently it was the largest group of Americans to return since the Vietnam War. Several of them were war veterans and their leader, a marine who was stationed near Hue, had received the VC. At the dinner he was seated next to an ex-Viet-Cong colonel who repeatedly put his arm round his former enemy's shoulders throughout the meal and confided that his marriage had broken up because he was away fighting for so long. Later the ex-marine told us that he felt overwhelmed by his return to Vietnam and commented, 'I never realised these guys got married,' as if in the madness of war he had not thought of the enemy as human.

When we entered the hotel lobby after our dinner on the terrace we were astonished to see yet another large group of ageing people dressed as mandarins, again processing to music, but this time they were French, and looked very uneasy in their costumes. At that moment the American group of mandarins came down the stairs, having finished their dinner. Seconds later, from outside the hotel entrance, there was a deafening sound of hundreds of firecrackers, set off by the hotel staff as a celebration of both reunions. Dense smoke began surging into the hotel lobby. 'Gracious heavens,' cried an old American woman, 'What the hell is this, what about our hearing?' while others shrieked in alarm, clearly wondering if the war had started again. Shouts of *'Mon Dieu, qu'est-ce qui se passe?'* came from the French mandarins. The smoke got thicker and both groups of mandarins bumped into each other in the lobby. All we could see were the shapes of bodies groping around in panic, while the music that had accompanied the procession blared on and the firecrackers continued. By now Elizabeth and I were hysterical with laughter, unable to believe the bizarre scene we were witnessing in the kitsch surroundings of this broken down hotel.

Tue took us to two places, both in shacks, to try culinary specialities of Hue. The first (pictured right) sold only three things: *banh beo*, *bahn loc* and *bahn nam*, all served in tiny portions, less than a mouthful, and eaten many at a time. Served in miniature bowls, *bahn beo* consisted of a jellyish paste, made from sticky rice flour, sprinkled with crumbled dried shrimp, dried pork crackling and a trickle of chilli fish sauce. *Banh loc* was a steamed small banana leaf parcel filled with a mixture of whole dried shrimp encased in a jelly of glutinous manioc root. My favourite, *bahn nam*, was also a steamed banana leaf parcel; inside was a sticky rice paste sprinkled with dried shrimps and infused with the subtle flavour of the banana leaf wrapping.

The other establishment was run by a family, all of whom were deaf and dumb. Their Hue speciality was a small omelette – fried until crispy and then filled with shrimp, pork and bean sprouts. To eat it, we tore off pieces of the omelette and added them to a bowl containing salad, mint leaves and a spiced sauce based on dried green bean – a lovely mixture of tastes and textures. The abundant use of salad leaves and herbs in every Vietnamese meal, always including mint, must surely also have been encouraged by the French love of salads. Perhaps the same is true of eating morning glory, or *convolvulus*, whose one-day peacock-blue flowers remind me of summer mornings in France.

We left the picturesque trading town of Hoi An at 5.30am to drive south down the coast to Nha Trang, the town where the last emperor of Vietnam, the self-indulgent Bao Dai, had a holiday villa from the 1920s until he abdicated in favour of Ho Chi Minh's Democratic

Republic of Vietnam in 1945. The journey took more than thirteen hours on a partly unmade road, passing through many villages and markets, and was in places incredibly beautiful. Green hills were a backdrop for electric-green paddy fields ripening to yellow, while on the coast side were miles of empty pristine beaches, islands out at sea and pretty bays. The villages had neat mud and palm leaf houses with little gardens ornamented by flower pots. In the busy markets, farmers and fishermen sold their produce, including dried sea horses, used for medicine. A full moon began to rise as we finally reached Nha Trang. There was no development in what is now one of Vietnam's main

resort towns, but we knew that Bao Dai's old holiday villa had been turned into a hotel. It seemed an ideal place for us to stay.

The hotel was in fact three white villas with turquoise blue shutters and gardens in between, built on a hillock with wonderful views on all sides, over the sea, coast and islands on three sides, and to the hills on the other. Inside the villas no imperial luxury remained. The rooms were large but shabby with ugly brown varnish coating any wood, bright blue gloss roughly painted on the walls, rickety furnishings and fluorescent tubes stuck anywhere because the 1930s light fittings no longer worked. But the rooms were glamorised by the heady smell of

Hue omelettes

The family who swiftly cooked and served these delicious omelettes from their shack in Hue did so silently, but with wide smiles. Since they couldn't explain how they made the omelettes, I could only watch, guess and experiment later. This is an ideal quick supper.

Serves 4

1–2 fresh red chillies

generous handful of coriander leaves

handful of mint leaves

225g cooked peeled prawns

2 heaped teaspoons Thai shrimp paste

100g bean sprouts

6 large free-range eggs

6 tablespoons cold water

groundnut oil for frying

sea salt

Cut open the chillies lengthways under running water and discard the seeds and stems, then slice crossways as finely as possible. Roughly chop the coriander and mint leaves, keeping them separate. Put the prawns into a bowl and mix in the shrimp paste. Have the bean sprouts ready.

Put a sheet of kitchen paper on each serving plate and place in a very low oven, to warm. For the omelettes, break the eggs into a bowl and mix lightly with a fork, then whisk in the water. Season with a little salt and stir in the chillies, together with 2 teaspoons of the chopped coriander.

Pour a 1cm depth of groundnut oil into a small frying pan and place over a high heat until smoking. Now pour in a quarter of the egg mixture and swirl to form a round. When the mixture has bubbled up right through to the centre and is very brown and crispy underneath, quickly pile a quarter of the prawns, bean sprouts, remaining coriander and mint on one side, then fold the omelette over to enclose the filling. Using a wide spatula, carefully transfer to one of the warmed paper-lined serving plates.

The omelettes should really be eaten straight away, but you can keep them warm in the oven while you cook the rest, then serve at once. Gently lift one side of the omelette with a spatula and ease the paper away from underneath before serving.

frangipani from large old trees outside, and by their views. The best were from what had been Bao Dai's bedroom – three large windows looked onto different and equally spectacular sea views – I wrote in my diary that they must be the best hotel views in the world.

On our first brightly moonlit evening, almost intoxicated by the smell of the frangipani, we watched silhouettes of fishermen going out in their boats for the night's fishing, and the slowly changing light as the full moon rose higher and turned the sea into a sparkling sheet of glass. In the distance were overlapping mountains in different shades of purple and blue.

The next morning we looked out to sea and noticed that many of the fishing boats had not returned to the shore and were close together in one place at sea. When we asked why, we were told that during the night smugglers had arrived with a boat full of television sets, but the police spotted them so they emptied their cargo into the sea. Now the fishermen were trying to bring up salt-corroded television sets, in the hope they might make them work again.

For three sun-filled days and moonlit nights we relaxed, swimming from the little beach beneath the villas, where we attracted a growing number of friendly local boys who crammed close to us under the only small umbrella as we tried to read. And we ate. In the town we found a restaurant lit by oil lamps where we dipped fine slivers of raw beef into a bowl of rice vinegar and onions bubbling over a charcoal stove and then wrapped the beef in rice paper with salad leaves and bean sprouts. On the street near the villas was a barbecue stall where they encased eel meat and pork in caul, a sort of Vietnamese faggot. And for lunch we sat on low stools beside stalls where they ladled broth and rice noodles into bowls with herbs and other additions we chose.

On the last balmy evening at Bao Dai villas we were alone on the

terrace under a canopy made from an American silk parachute, which undulated gently like waves in the soft breeze. We marvelled yet again at the view of sea and islands, and had another delicately cooked meal. There was a mouth-watering tamarind crab, shrimp and squid hotpot into which we threw the usual handfuls of fresh leaves and mint. And tender eel that had been marinated in sesame oil, rice vinegar, lemon grass and chilli was grilled at a brazier on our table and served with morning glory. The finale, *che*, was an unlikely sweet made from the first crop of tender sweetcorn and topped with coconut cream; it turned out to be irresistible. The potent smell of frangipani scented the night air.

Sweetcorn surprise

Variations of this sweet soup – *che* – are sold on the streets of Vietnam, in special *che* cafés, and in restaurants. This is my interpretation of the one we ate looking out to sea from the last emperor's villas; it's the kind of sweet comfort food I find hard to resist. I use the extra-sweet type of frozen sweetcorn. Glutinous (or sticky) rice flour and coconut milk powder are obtainable from oriental food stores.

Serves 4–6

25g glutinous rice flour

500ml water

75g caster sugar

1 level teaspoon salt

275g frozen 'supersweet' sweetcorn, thawed

For the coconut cream:

230ml hot water

100g coconut milk powder

sea salt

Put the glutinous rice flour into a saucepan, add 100ml of the water and stir until smooth. Then gradually stir in the remaining 400ml water, followed by the caster sugar and salt. Place the saucepan over a fairly high heat and bring the mixture to the boil, stirring constantly with a wooden spoon. Reduce the heat slightly and allow to bubble for 2 minutes, still stirring.

Remove the pan from the heat and stir in the sweetcorn. Pour the mixture into glass serving bowls. Leave to cool, then cover and chill in the fridge.

Meanwhile, make the coconut cream. Pour the hot water into a mixing bowl, sprinkle in the coconut milk powder, add a pinch of salt and whisk until smooth. Allow to cool, then cover and chill thoroughly in the fridge. Before serving, spoon the coconut cream gently over the sweetcorn, showing some of the yellow corn pudding.

Marble temples in the sky

'Before landing,' a gentle Indian voice announced over the intercom on our flight to Gujarat, 'we shall be serving heavy snacks', but the little vegetable samosas were crisp and delicate, not heavy at all. Delicacy is what I remember when I think of the food of Gujarat, India's westernmost state. The predominant religion is Jain, an ancient sect that preaches non-violence and respect for all living beings, including insects. As a consequence, an exquisite and unique vegetarian cuisine has developed due to strict rules: only the leaves, seeds and beans of vegetables can be eaten, not the roots as insects might be killed in the digging up. The successful business community in Gujarat evolved because Jains became traders, since farming involved killing animals. Of all Indians, they are the most protective of the cow and never wear leather. Jain monks even tie gauze over their mouths to prevent inadvertently swallowing flies, and they don't eat after 5pm because of the evening rush of insects in the air. They also bandage their feet

*Johnny on the road,
trying out another
famous form of
Gujarati transport.*

to avoid crushing crawling things and they even sweep the ground in front of them as they walk to clear it of any living creature.

One of the reasons I have visited India more than anywhere else is that each area is almost like a different country, yet with familiarities. Because of its food and religion, Gujarat stands truly alone. Although 2005 was my third visit in twenty years, for Johnny – who now shares my life and travels – it was a first, and I was eager to share it with him. More than anything I wanted to return to Palitana (pictured right), the most sacred place of pilgrimage for the Jains. A walled city of more than one thousand white marble temples of all sizes, it was built for the gods over nine hundred years ago at the top of the holy mountain of Shatrunjaya. Almost two decades before, my children had thought this gleaming city of intricately carved, domed buildings looked like a magic kingdom in a Disney film, and half expected a fairy to fly over it and create sparkling stars in the sky with her wand.

Johnny and I stayed at a 'heritage' home-stay, Vijay Vilas, near the foot of the mountain. Built as a country house in 1906, it was handsome but dilapidated, and partly ruined as the result of a past cyclone, a hurricane and the recent earthquake in Gujarat, but it was evocative of a lost past and very peaceful. We arrived at sunset and were welcomed by the endearing family who owned the house, members of the Gujarat royal family, the Singhs: Yashpal, an exceptionally tall, clever man; his pretty wife Nitya; their one-year-old daughter Vishwambari; and his mother Bagwati, who cooked supper for us. The meal included a delicious dish of spicy spinach and fried eggs – very fresh from the chickens that wandered about outside.

We had to start early the next day for our climb up to the temples, as it takes up to two hours to ascend the five thousand stone steps up the mountain. Fortunately we were distracted from the length and steepness of the climb by increasingly lovely views over the surrounding country and hills, and by the characters we met coming up and down. There were pilgrims of all ages, men wrapped in white cotton with long wooden sticks, monks with masks round their mouths and pads on their feet, Gujarati businessmen in suits, and whole families together, any elderly or disabled person being carried up on a doli – a flat seat hung from two wooden poles. Many of the pilgrims stay in lodgings for

Spicy spinach with eggs and chickpeas

The most usual combination of spices in Gujarati cooking is ground coriander and cumin seeds. This is my version of one of the simple but delicious dishes we enjoyed at Palitana before our climb up the holy mountain. It can be rustled up quickly and served with some heated chapatis or nan bread for a complete and healthy supper.

Serves 4

1kg spinach

5–6cm piece fresh root ginger

3 large cloves garlic

2 fresh red chillies

50g butter

3–4 tablespoons groundnut oil

2 heaped teaspoons ground coriander

1 heaped teaspoon ground cumin

400g tin chickpeas, drained

2 tablespoons lemon juice

4 medium free-range eggs

2 rounded teaspoons mustard seeds

sea salt, black pepper

Warm a large, fairly shallow serving dish (ideally round), in a low oven. Wash the spinach thoroughly and remove the stems. Peel the ginger and garlic and chop together finely. Cut the chillies open lengthways under running water, discard the seeds and stems, then finely slice crossways.

Bring a little water to the boil in a large saucepan. Add the spinach, cover and cook for only a minute or two until just wilted, stirring a few times. Drain the spinach and press out any excess liquid, then chop fairly small.

Melt half of the butter with 1 tablespoon of the groundnut oil in a large, deep frying pan or a saucepan over a medium heat. Add the ginger and garlic, chillies and ground spices, and stir around for a minute or two. Reduce the heat and add the chopped spinach, chickpeas, lemon juice and remaining butter. Stir around over the low heat for about 5 minutes. Season to taste with salt, and a little pepper if the chilli doesn't provide enough heat for you. Spread the mixture out evenly in the warmed serving dish.

Add another 2 tablespoons groundnut oil to the pan and fry the eggs, two at a time, over a fairly high heat, basting with the oil until the white is only just set. Using a slotted spatula, lift out the eggs and place them on the bed of spinach. Add the mustard seeds to the oil remaining in the pan, adding a spoonful more oil if there doesn't appear to be enough. Heat until the seeds pop, then tip directly onto the eggs and spinach. Serve at once.

a week or more at the bottom of the mountain, eating one meal a day at the same time in the same place in just five minutes. Some climbed, often running, up to the temples and down again twice a day, and were very thin from fasting. One old man, emaciated yet walking quickly uphill, told us he had fasted for ninety-nine days.

Now and then young girls with cropped hair, dressed in white, skipped cheerfully down the steps towards us, chatting to each other and giggling girlishly. A passing pilgrim told us they were 'saints' – girls who had given up everything to devote themselves to religion, or whose families had decided they would become saints when they were

as young as eight years old. They had no money and nowhere to live but people took them in and fed them.

Eventually at the top of the mountain we reached a high wall and saw temples beyond. An extremely large businessman who had been carried up on a doli was arguing angrily over the price of flowers for temple offerings, while four small, skinny men – each had carried one end of a pole and manoeuvred his great weight up the mountain – looked on, still breathless and shining with sweat, waiting for their payment. Outside the entrance, groups of women and girls in bright tribal clothes were selling yogurt in shallow earthenware dishes

(pictured left), either sprinkled with *gur*, the caramel-flavoured unrefined sugar, or with salt and spices. Each woman urged us to buy her yogurt, assuring us it was the best. Made from buffalo milk, the yogurt was creamy rich and so thick you could cut it with a knife. Beside the city of the gods the taste was fittingly ambrosial, and wonderfully refreshing after our climb.

There was a cheerful atmosphere of achievement at the summit, but I was disturbed to see tribal women toiling up the mountain in the blazing sun, leading donkeys laden with building materials for repairing the temples (pictured on page 206); they did this countless times a day.

Within the walls, Palitana looked like a celestial city in a fairy story. On a series of hills, as far as we could see, there were hundreds of perfectly preserved and intricately carved temples, from huge to tiny – all spotlessly clean in the Jain way. Sweepers were constantly at work, both inside the buildings and out, and temple keepers polished the marble gods with oil. Slim marble gods of every size, with satin-smooth white skin, long ears, heavy eyebrows and red lips, all sat in the same cross-legged position. Their bright eyes, made from jewels, shone out at us through the doorways and seemed to follow us as we passed by.

Later, in the main temple at the top of the hill, we saw large crowds praying and queuing up to touch the principal Jain god, Mahavira (pictured left), bringing their offerings of rice and fruits. The rice was arranged on the floor in symbolic patterns. Every afternoon at 3pm the god is adorned with jewels that are otherwise kept locked up, and each day the jewels must be arranged in a different way. The Jain gods are not fantasies like Hindu gods: they are called prophets and based on real people; Mahavara lived in the sixth century BC and was a contemporary of Gautama Buddha. 'The Jain god is an objective god,' said a man next to us as we watched the fascinating scene, 'he doesn't judge, praise or punish.' When we descended the mountain and finally reached the bottom, it felt as though we had come down to earth again, after being in another world amongst the temples in the sky. Before returning to Vijay Vilas, we bought a Jain rose petal jam, packed with translucent petals and dotted with saffron stamens too.

One morning, later in our journey, we saw a large elephant (pictured right) and several groups walking along the road ahead of us before turning off towards an extensive area of multi-coloured tents.

Our driver Kuman told us that these people were on a pilgrimage to Palitana, organised and paid for by rich Jains. There were eight hundred pilgrims of all ages. They walked barefoot for eighteen kilometres a day starting at 5am, though the tents, bedding, luggage, food and cooks went ahead of them in trucks to the next overnight stop. And they had the occasional day of rest, such as the one we had stumbled on. We were received enthusiastically by a group of Jain priests, female as well as male, who invited us to lunch. In one enormous tent we found a scene of extreme jollity and loud laughter; hundreds of people squatted

Gujarat aubergines and tomatoes

Aubergines and tomatoes are a popular combination in many of the countries I have visited. Even if you are not cooking an Indian meal, this dish is good as an accompaniment to fish or chicken, as part of a vegetarian meal, or even as a pasta sauce.

Serves 6

3 large aubergines

3 medium onions

2–3 fresh red chillies

600g small ripe tomatoes

3 tablespoons groundnut oil

2 rounded teaspoons mustard seeds

1 level teaspoon fennel seeds

2 rounded teaspoons ground coriander

1 level teaspoon ground cumin

1 level teaspoon ground turmeric

1 teaspoon caster sugar

5 tablespoons water

small bunch of coriander, trimmed

sea salt, black pepper

Heat the grill to its highest setting. Cut the aubergines in half lengthways and grill them, skin side up, close to the heat source, until the skins have blackened and cracked, and the flesh inside is very soft.

Meanwhile, peel, quarter and thinly slice the onions. Cut open the chillies lengthways under running water, remove the seeds and stems and finely slice the flesh crossways. Halve or quarter the tomatoes, according to size.

Scoop the flesh out of the blackened aubergine skins with a metal spoon. Chop the flesh roughly, crumbling on a small piece of the blackened skin.

Heat the groundnut oil in a large, deep frying pan over a fairly high heat, add the sliced onions and stir around until well browned. Then add the mustard seeds, fennel seeds and sliced chillies and stir for another 2–3 minutes before sprinkling in the ground coriander, cumin and turmeric.

Now add the tomatoes, sugar and water, and continue to stir over the heat for 3–4 minutes until the tomatoes begin to soften. Add the chopped aubergine flesh and season with salt and pepper to taste. Cover the pan, reduce the heat and leave for a minute or two to reheat the aubergines.

Wash the coriander, pat dry and tear the leaves from the stalks. Chop the stalks, stir into the aubergine mixture and cook for a minute or two. Chop the leaves roughly; stir most of them into the mixture too. Transfer to a heated serving dish and sprinkle the remaining coriander leaves on top.

in long rows at low tables eating Gujarati thalis with gusto. Like many westerners I find it hard to squat comfortably on the ground and I moved about awkwardly next to a large lady, who was totally at ease. But the thali was well worth the discomfort.

On large leaves, sewn together with grass (pictured left), were fine slices of sweet purple onions, scarlet tomatoes, slices of red carrot, raw beetroot, cucumbers and sprouting mug dal. And tiny dishes were continually refilled with mung dal curry; charred aubergines and sweet tomatoes; a red chilli and garlic chutney; a mildly spiced purée of green vegetables; rice, lentils and peas with a burnt, crispy top; and chickpeas fried with salt, peanut flour and chilli.

Most savoury dishes in Gujarat are slightly sweetened, but there is a great variety of sweet dishes too, eaten at the same time as the savoury ones, not afterwards. That day we had *sukri*, made from wheat, palm sugar and ghee, and syrupy golden *jelebis*. White buffalo butter was served in clay pots, and we drank buffalo buttermilk sprinkled with salt and cumin.

As we left, feeling as large as these hefty pilgrims, Kuman told us that he often drove Jains and that they were always very cheerful. He, however, did not seem at all happy that day; he was worried about his eighteen-year-old daughter, who was nine months pregnant by her penniless twenty-year-old husband. It would be Kuman's first grandchild, and his daughter had been told, despite being young and healthy with no complications, that she would have a Caesarean that day. This shocking practice was happening to countless poor families who did not know better, simply for the monetary gain and convenience of the doctor. Kuman said the operation would cost the equivalent of £200, a fortune for him, and would mean the same for any of his daughter's future pregnancies.

When we stopped in a town for lunch he went to ring and find out how the operation had gone. He walked slowly back to the car and when we asked apprehensively how his daughter and the baby were, he replied that they were both well, but he looked devastated. The baby was a girl. 'Girls are very costly,' said Kuman, 'they can't make money when they grow up and they need money to get married.' At the end of our journey we went to the one small room where Kuman lived in a slum quarter of Ahmedabad. His daughter lay on some quilts,

Fresh coriander chutney with coconut

Excellent fresh chutneys are always part of Gujarati meals and this is one of my favourites. In Gujarat they use grated fresh coconut, which you may find here in Thai grocers, or you can buy a whole coconut if you are up to breaking it open and grating it. But soaked desiccated coconut works here and makes the recipe quick and easy. The chutney keeps well in a covered container in the fridge for several days and is lovely in sandwiches.

Serves about 6

200g unsweetened desiccated coconut

1 large bunch of coriander

2-4 fresh green or red chillies, to taste

juice of 1 lime

1 teaspoon crushed sea salt

1 teaspoon cumin seeds

1 rounded teaspoon sesame seeds

Put the desiccated coconut in a bowl, pour on sufficient warm water to cover and leave on one side while you prepare the other ingredients. Wash the coriander thoroughly, remove only the base of the stalks, pat dry with kitchen paper and cut up roughly. Cut open the chillies lengthways under running water and discard the seeds and stems.

Drain the soaked coconut and squeeze it dry with kitchen paper. Put the coconut into a food processor with the coriander and chillies, lime juice and salt. Whiz until the chutney is as smooth as possible.

Turn into a bowl, stir in the cumin and sesame seeds, cover with cling film and keep in the fridge until ready to serve.

looking tired and expressionless. Slightly apart from her was a thin little baby with kohl-rimmed eyes; the young mother did not look at or hold the baby.

We had been told that the poor often don't feed their girl babies enough; in a photograph we were shown of a mother with twins – a boy and a girl – the boy was chubby and smiling, while the girl looked as if she was wasting away. I remembered how the servants in our house in Syria in 1953 couldn't understand why my mother was so sad to have lost her baby daughter, and I feared for that little dark girl in the shack in Gujarat.

Mount Girnar, which rises dramatically from the flat, dry plains of Saurashtra, is the highest peak in Gujarat. Both Jain and Hindu pilgrims climb up ten thousand steps to temples built for the gods on five hills at the top. At the base we found a teeming, shouting mass of religious and commercial activity with stalls selling food, holy pictures, offerings for the gods and much more. A group of poor pilgrims who had travelled for days in a rusty bus with their bedding and cooking utensils were huddled over fires cooking *dal batis*. These flour and water patties – filled with a mung dal and chilli liquid – looked like blackened tennis balls. The patties were sealed over the flames of the fire, buried in the hot ashes for fifteen minutes, then broken open; the pilgrims added ghee before eating them hungrily.

We only walked up a short way to visit one of the naked Jain sadhus who sit completely still beside whitewashed shrines. As we entered a quiet courtyard we saw the sadhu, Bibi Shantaben, sitting cross-legged on a low stool in a small open room on the other side, attended by a pretty young girl and boy who were both fourteen years old. There was a feeling of calm and all three smiled warmly at us. Bibi was fifty-nine years old and had been a naked guru since he was twelve. He had been in this place for twenty-eight years, where he sat all day and slept on the stone floor in the courtyard at night. Seeing me rub an aching leg, he asked the girl to fetch him some large leaves impregnated with oil, which he assured me would cure my ache. The girl then tore up some bandages and tied the leaves round my leg. At this point a pilgrim prostrated herself before the naked sadhu and asked for a book. Without covering himself, the sadhu got up and dangled past us to fetch the book, and a photograph of himself with two other naked sadhus. I never knew if the oily leaves worked; they fell off my leg soon after we left the genial guru.

The mansions of the ghost town of Sidphur in northern Gujarat contrasted with the marble temples of the Jains. It was as if we had been transported to a semi-European film set. During the late nineteenth century the Dawoodi Bohras, a Muslim sect, were an affluent merchant

Johnny and me with the naked sadhu, covering himself with the photograph.

Khandvi

In Ahmedabad I met Mrs Nanavati, who showed me how to prepare and cook khandvi, which could be described as a sort of delicate Indian pasta. The 'pasta' is made from a paste of chickpea flour, used in many Gujarati dishes, and yogurt. Golden with turmeric, it is transformed into little rolls and served cold, scattered with coriander leaves and the typically Gujarati garnish of seeds popped in oil – sometimes with a little grated fresh coconut too. I often serve khandvi as the first course of a non-Indian meal, or as part of a vegetarian Indian spread. You can buy gram (chickpea) flour at oriental stores.

Serves 6–8

100g gram (chickpea) flour

1 teaspoon salt

½ level teaspoon chilli powder

½ rounded teaspoon ground turmeric

walnut-sized piece fresh root ginger

2 tablespoons whole milk yogurt

600ml water

groundnut oil for oiling

For the garnish:

2 tablespoons groundnut oil

1 level teaspoon cumin seeds

2 level teaspoons mustard seeds

1 rounded teaspoon sesame seeds

1 tablespoon unsweetened desiccated coconut

handful of coriander leaves

Sift the gram flour, salt, chilli powder and turmeric into a mixing bowl. Peel and roughly chop the ginger, then press in a garlic crusher held over the flour mixture to extract the juice only. Put the yogurt into a jug, add the water and whisk or stir thoroughly. Gradually add this liquid to the flour mixture, stirring with a wooden spoon and whisking if necessary until the mixture is smooth.

Pour the mixture into a heavy-based saucepan (preferably non-stick) and place over a medium heat. When it begins to bubble, reduce the heat to as low as possible and stir continually until the mixture is very thick; this can take about 25 minutes. Remove from the heat.

Lightly oil two or three large flat baking sheets – or any other smooth flat surface. Spread the thick paste over the oiled surfaces as thinly as you can – the thinner the better; ideally you should be almost able to see through the paste. Leave for a few minutes until cold and set, then cut into strips, about 3cm wide and 8cm long. Roll up lightly into little Swiss rolls.

Arrange the khandvi on a serving plate, or perhaps on individual plates if you are having them as a first course. Unless serving quite soon, cover with cling film and refrigerate, for up to a day.

Take the khandvi from the fridge about an hour before serving. Prepare the garnish just before you eat: heat the groundnut oil in a frying pan over a fairly high heat and add the cumin and mustard seeds; when these begin to pop (almost immediately), stir in the sesame seeds and remove from the heat. Spoon the garnish over the khandvi and sprinkle with the coconut. Roughly chop the coriander leaves and throw them on top.

community in Sidphur, trading mostly in ironware. They built streets of tall, majestic buildings (pictured right), painted in pastel colours, with fluted pillars, ornately carved windows, elaborate plasterwork, intricate stonework and balconies with fretwork awnings.

In the first half of the twentieth century many of the Sidphur Bohras moved away to trade all over the world. Now their grand mansions were almost all empty and the dust roads of the wide streets deserted. Just a few ageing members of the Bohra community remained, usually living in one room while the rest of the house decayed around them. It was an extraordinary sight and atmosphere, especially as beyond was the noisy modern town of Sidphur, crammed with hooting cars, motorbikes, people, animals and carts.

When David and I visited Sidphur in 1986 with our children, the Bohra area already seemed abandoned, but in one house we found an old man wearing a red brocade waistcoat and flared turquoise trousers. This was Mr Harawala (pictured above), alias 'Professor Obre – International Rocket Magician'. Rococo mirrors carved in teak hung on the walls of every large dust-covered room of the five-storey house, together with faded posters for the magician's performances. Girls in bikinis were portrayed saying, 'Please don't look at me – see Professor Obre's magic show', and, 'Oh my God, how sweet performance tonight'. 'The Great Obre' showed our son some of his tricks, including 'Perspiration into Perfume'. Henry was in heaven.

Towards the end of our journey we came to Danta, a small town in a colourful tribal area set amongst the beautiful Aravalli Hills, which are forested with flowering trees and full of exotic birds and wild animals. Our host was the Maharana of Danta, a distinguished-looking tall man with pale green eyes, an aquiline nose and a splendid moustache. The Maharana's house looked onto the old palace of his forebears and the hills beyond and he offered it as a home-stay. His passions were his

fine Marwari horses, descended from the war horses of feudal India, as well as four Basset hounds, a Great Dane, the wildlife he lived amongst, and cricket. On our first morning the Maharana came to our room in his cricket jersey, bringing some binoculars. Later his son, who shared his father's passion for cricket, was to take us in a jeep to some of the tribal villages.

The Maharana sat with us on our balcony sharing our breakfast of warm chapatis, thick yogurt with local forest honey, and little lemony bananas. As we looked out at the wooded hill opposite and the old palace, with dozens of monkeys leaping about on its roof, birds swooped low and antelopes danced across the

The golden favourite

Gujarat is awash with sweet shops, displaying beautiful arrangements of yellow and white sweetmeats, many made with reduced milk, flavoured with saffron and cardamom. As the finale to almost every meal we were offered the yogurt-based shrikhand, a Gujarati speciality that is more of a dessert. Scattered with pomegranate seeds and pistachios, Mrs Nanavati's shrikhand was light and soothing, and not too sweet. I was determined to create my own version; by adding soft white cheese I was able to avoid the usual first step of draining the yogurt through muslin for several hours. It tastes lovely.

Serves 4

3 tablespoons whole milk

4 generous pinches of saffron strands

seeds from 4–5 cardamom pods

250g full-fat soft cheese

350g Greek style yogurt

3 tablespoons icing sugar

3 rounded tablespoons pomegranate seeds

4 rounded teaspoons nibbed or chopped pistachio nuts

Put the milk and saffron in a small pan and bring just to the boil. Stir to distribute the saffron, remove from the heat and leave on one side. Crush the cardamom seeds, using a pestle and mortar.

Put the soft cheese into a bowl, add the yogurt and stir to mix roughly together. Sift in the icing sugar and sprinkle in the ground cardamom. Whisk the mixture thoroughly until very smooth, then gradually whisk in the cooled saffron milk.

Spoon the mixture into 4 small glass bowls and chill in the fridge for an hour or more. You can keep the dessert in the fridge for several hours or until the next day.

Before serving, straight from the fridge, sprinkle the pomegranate seeds and chopped pistachios over each serving.

scene. 'Listen,' said the Maharana, and we heard the alarm call of a peacock followed by the 'ugh, ugh' alert noise of monkeys. 'That means there's a leopard close by,' the Maharana explained. We borrowed the binoculars and spotted the proud beast, sitting in a tree with a monkey on a branch above looking down at him. The Maharana seemed as thrilled as we were.

The next morning, when I woke to the sounds of birds and animals in the forest, and the sun making patterns through the curtains, I realised that it is only when I travel that I start the day with the same feeling of simple excitement that I used to get as a child, my head clear of any mundane worries or responsibilities. To me it is more rejuvenating than anything else, and I hope I can experience a wide variety of places, food, people and surprises for many more years.

Index

Acknowledgements

My journey through this book would not have been such a pleasurable experience without the input and encouragement of several invaluable 'travelling companions'. I would like to thank my agent Araminta Whitley and her colleague Peta Nightingale for believing in the idea from the start; Jane O'Shea at Quadrille for agreeing, with reassuring support, to publish a rather different book; Clare Lattin for realising that it would have something for everyone; my meticulous editor Janet Illsley, whose enthusiasm made it seem as if she was enjoying each adventure and meal as much as I had; Jason Lowe, who was able to make his mouth-watering photographs of the recipes blend so perfectly with my old pictures, together with each era and every place; Louisa Carter who made recreating the dishes in my kitchen a relaxed joy; and designer extraordinaire Lawrence Morton who has so cleverly created an exciting, romantic and beautiful-looking book.

I am also happy to have re-lived times with travelling companions past and present; I'm grateful to Hubert and Fidelity, my stepbrother and stepsister, who contributed some early memories and photographs of Syria and Peru, to several friends who reminded me of shared moments long past, and to all the characters I met in different parts of the world, many of whom feature in my stories, or cooked food which provided inspiration for my recipes. Thanks too are due to my son Henry, with whom I share a passion for food, for giving me a burst of confidence at the beginning by saying 'Mum, this book will be your best!' As often, my daughters Liza and Kate, and a few close friends, bore patiently with my frequent overexcitement and occasional deadline panic. And of course I am indebted to Johnny for sharing every step of the way, reading the first draft of each chapter, tasting every dish and making me feel I was taking the right path.

Publishing director Jane O'Shea
Creative director Helen Lewis
Project editor Janet Illsley
Art direction & design Lawrence Morton
Photographer Jason Lowe
Food stylist Louisa Carter
Production Ruth Deary, Vincent Smith

First published in 2010 by
Quadrille Publishing Limited
Alhambra House, 27–31 Charing
Cross Road, London WC2H 0LS
www.quadrille.co.uk

Text © 2010 Josceline Dimbleby
Photography © 2010 Jason Lowe
Design and layout © 2010 Quadrille
Publishing Limited

Cataloguing in Publication Data: a catalogue record for this book is available from the British Library.

ISBN 978 184400 848 3

Printed in China